MANAGING TODAY'S CHURCH

Robert N. White, editor

Judson Press® Valley Forge

MANAGING TODAY'S CHURCH

Copyright © 1981
Judson Press, Valley Forge, Pa 19481

Library of Congress Cataloging in Publication Data
Main entry under title:

Managing today's church.

    Bibliography: p.
    Includes index.
    1. Church management—Addresses, essays, lectures. I. White, Robert N.
BV652.M358   254   81-5783
ISBN 0-8170-0871-3   AACR2

The name JUDSON PRESS is registered as a trademark in the U.S. Patent Office.
Printed in the U.S.A. ⊕

Acknowledgments

The pastors participating in our many seminar sessions shaped many of the ideas in this book. We thank them for their enthusiastic interest in these discussions. Our associations with these pastors are a rewarding part of our seminar work.

Our thanks go to Glenn Rayle, who contributed greatly in the editing process, and to Phyllis Harper and Imelda Dunbar who endured through many retypings.

Robert N. White
Peter R. Peacock
Robert W. Shively
Jack D. Ferner

Contents

Introduction

Administering a church involves congregational leaders in wrestling with perplexing and frustrating problems. This book is designed to help ministers and lay leaders. It is written out of a conviction that church organizations can be managed effectively to achieve their objectives.

The management concepts we have set forth here have proved sound in both profit-making and not-for-profit organizations. We have applied these concepts specifically to administrative issues that arise in churches. The book is designed to acquaint ministers and lay leaders with the methods other organizations use to solve their administrative problems. These methods can enable pastors and lay leaders to work together in solving problems and allocating the resources of the church most efficiently in pursuit of reasonable goals.

How This Book Came to Be Written

This book comes out of five years of dialogue between professors of management and more than 250 pastors (and some lay leaders) since 1973. Starting in that year the Babcock Graduate School of Management, of Wake Forest University in Winston-Salem, North Carolina, began a series of church management seminars. Once or twice a year since then we have held week-long seminars involving thirty to thirty-five participants. Pastors now come to the Wake Forest campus for this seminar from all over the eastern half of the United States. Participants uniformly leave the seminar praising the practicality and pertinence of the concepts presented.

The seminar faculty members, who are the authors of this book, are not only well-qualified educators but also have had extensive practical experience in administrative organizations. Most of the faculty members are also lay leaders in their respective churches.

Review of the current literature indicates that there are few books specifically about church management and none with this particular table of contents. While some of these topics are covered in other texts, we believe the perspective that has grown out of the relationship of experienced management teachers and knowledge-able pastors working together is unique. Our seminar participants have in effect defined the contents of the book by their own concerns. Before each seminar starts, we survey participants about their concerns. As a result, we feel confident that the issues presented here are the issues that pastors and other church leaders want help on.

This book is presented in a "how to" style. We offer practical guidelines, step-by-step processes, and illustrations of how to put ideas into practice.

A Perspective on the Contents of This Book

Management is a very broad topic. This book has as its ambitious purpose the presentation of management fundamentals in a church environment. A brief overview of what is discussed and the logic of including the topics will be helpful to the reader.

First, the management role and duties of the pastor are examined. How can this role be clarified and defined? How can performance be evaluated?

Next is the planning for the future of the church. Such a planning process includes strategic planning, short-term planning, and annual financial management and planning. Due to the different types of managerial expertise involved, we have chosen to deal with each of these areas separately (chapters 2, 3, and 4 respectively). In concurrence with current organizational trends we have also chosen to separate the responsibilities for planning from those of financial management.

The distinctions and interrelationships pertaining to these topics can be briefly summarized as follows:

1. Strategic planning (chapter 2) sets long-term objectives for

growth and change and specifies how the church plans to meet these objectives.

2. Short-term plans (chapter 3). These spell out annual objectives and required action steps for individual church programs. The emphasis in this chapter is, however, on the logic of program objectives and activities—the who, what, why issues.
3. The annual financial plan (chapter 4) focuses on translating the strategic and short-term plans into financial terms of revenues and costs. Emphasis is on the one-year budget as it pertains to translating all programs and nonprogram functions of the church into financial practicality.

Marketing of the church (chapter 5), a controversial topic, is explained in candid, specific terms. This chapter presents concepts which, to our knowledge, have not been addressed in other published books or articles. The marketing concept is accepted and applied in most successful expanding organizations (profit and nonprofit) today. Can the marketing concept be utilized in a church?

A church is people management by people. Thus the human resource is the focus of chapters 6, 7, and 8. First, personnel policies and practices in recruiting, hiring, and compensating employees are examined. Then the complex issues of motivating people to contribute effectively and harmoniously to church programs are discussed in chapters 7 and 8. A framework of motivational theory is delineated. Why do people perform or not perform in organizational environments? How can they become involved? What conditions are most conducive to increased motivation? How can the pastor motivate volunteer personnel?

The next chapter, "The Administrative Audit," presents a concept not often practiced in churches. It stems from the premise that any organization needs a periodic reevaluation of "how we are doing." If we adopted planning as a way of managing, are we getting desired results? Are we using people and money efficiently? Are our programs meeting targets? This is management in a stewardship context—checking up on management of our resources to ensure that we are getting results.

The final chapter is about time management. In our seminars for pastors this is such a popular topic that, while it doesn't deal with the

management of the church organization, we felt it should be
included for the pastors' personal benefit. The author of this
chapter has written a book and lectured extensively on time
management. His chapter tailors concepts especially to the pastor's
pressing problems of using limited time efficiently.

Our Hope

If ministers and lay leaders read this book together, we believe it
will provide solutions to the common management problems of
their churches, large and small. When their resources of time,
talent, and treasure are used to maximum effectiveness, the real
work of serving the Lord can assume its rightful top place in the list
of priorities of those entrusted with church leadership and
stewardship.

Chapter 1

The Pastor's Role As Manager

Where does the pastor fit in the organizational structure of the local church?

From conversations with hundreds of ministers and lay leaders I know that this question often perplexes and frustrates both groups. It is perplexing to pastors who must feel their way in their individual church environment in order to define for themselves a niche that is acceptable to the lay leadership. It is frustrating for lay leaders who are accustomed to the well-defined organizational structures of their companies.

Is the pastor the chief executive officer of the church? Or is the pastor first among equals, the equals being the wardens, deacons, or elders? Or is the pastor somewhere in the middle, taking directions from lay leadership on some matters and asserting leadership in others? Many pastors say they are in the middle, and it's no fun.

Any textbook on organizational effectiveness will tell you that a clear definition of executive authority and responsibility within the organizational framework is essential. Yet this kind of clarity and definition seems to be missing in church organizations with respect to the person at the top, the pastor. Let's go back to basic management concepts and organization theory to see if we can find some guidelines for dealing with this common church management issue.

What Is the Manager's Role?

According to basic managerial theory managers are involved in a policy process. That is, within their assigned sphere of responsibility they either formulate or implement the appropriate policy and sometimes do both. Managers also function within an organizational framework. They are responsible for a segment of the organization, such as a department, a section, or a division. Furthermore, they coordinate their unit with other components of the organization to ensure progress toward the overall goals of the enterprise.

The managerial process provides a description of what managers do. The process includes planning, organizing, staffing, directing, leading, communicating, and controlling. The techniques used in the managerial process will vary according to the size, complexity, and sophistication of the enterprise itself.

Managers' work is measurable in terms of results, both their own results and those of their subordinates.

Do These Apply to a Pastor?

These concepts tell us what managers do. Do they apply to what pastors do? Let's compare:

1. Pastors are involved in formulating and implementing administrative policies of the church.
2. Pastors engage in all of the elements identified as components of the management process, but their involvement varies with the individual church situation, their personal management style, and the working arrangement they have with lay leadership.
3. Pastors' work is measurable in terms of results to some extent. In many churches the administrative responsibilities are diffused among various committees. The pastors' responsibilities for these activities, as well as their relationship to the various committees, are often ill-defined. It may be difficult, therefore, to measure their accomplishments in some administrative areas.

So we find that applying conventional managerial theory to the pastor's role doesn't give us clear-cut answers. Why is this?

One clue is that a clear definition of the authority of the pastor is not always desired. This attitude may or may not be valid, but it exists nonetheless. Leaving some "gray area" around the pastor's authority and responsibility seems to cushion the conflicts that arise when a pastor asserts himself or herself to get things done in the church.

Also some pastors enjoy managing; others do not. The person's individual interests and capabilities influence the particular administrative role and managerial style the person adopts. When a pastor's decision-making role is not clearly defined, the lay leadership may move in and fill the gap, back off to avoid infringements on the pastor's perceived authority, or simply flounder helplessly and wonder why the church can't be run like a business.

A final clue may lie in an interesting aspect of the church as an organization—the fact that the goals of a church are never fully realized. In a business it is expected that both short-term and long-term goals will, to some reasonable degree, be achieved according to a timetable and that a new set of targets will then be adopted. But the church is different. Its basic mission is to keep striving until Christ has come again.

All these factors may contribute to a kind of haziness about the pastor's role as manager. But despite these problems effective church functioning requires that a wide variety of administrative tasks be well managed.

In this book we examine the central managerial tasks of the church, including planning, marketing, financial management, human resources management, and others. We explore how a church can approach each of these tasks in an effective manner. In each area we note that the extent to which the pastor assumes responsibility will vary from church to church.

What we have discussed thus far with respect to the pastor's managerial role simply confirms the difficulty of prescribing a set management posture that can apply to any pastor. Nonetheless, pastors must define their particular role in their current church in an acceptable manner. When no effort is made to define who is responsible for what, the result is inefficiency and conflict.

Let's examine an approach whereby any pastor and the governing board of the church can work together to define an appropriate managerial role for that particular pastor in that particular situation, with provisions for continued monitoring and adjustment of the role to meet changing circumstances. The suggested approach has the merits of objectivity, open communication, and clarification of issues without posing any threats to the pastor.

As outlined here, this approach can be used by pastor and board to improve their effectiveness at any time during the pastor's tenure in the church. Also a church board or pulpit committee may want to work through the process with a candidate or a new pastor so that both parties may come to a common understanding of what will be the pastor's role in the management of the church.

Defining the Pastor's Job[1]

What does a pastor do? How should he or she go about the job? What results should he or she achieve?

Questions like these are guaranteed to start an argument between pastor and lay leaders, within the lay leadership, or even between pastors, for that matter. However, finding an acceptable way of answering them is important to a healthy relationship between a pastor and the lay leadership.

The answers are particularly important in the early years of a pastor's service in a church. In the beginning expectations are being adjusted to reality on both sides. But too often lack of communication about expectations—of the pastor or the lay leaders—leads to dissatisfaction or to resignation to an unhappy situation for years to come.

This problem concerned me as chairman of the board of deacons in our small church. After an extensive search by our pulpit committee, a young minister was hired to replace a much-loved older man who had left us. Naturally the new man embarked on his new assignment with considerable uncertainty as to his responsibilities and authority. The governing board, not knowing the leadership capabilities or interests of their new pastor, was equally uncertain. Each expected the other to take charge.

The first year of the new pastor's call was particularly frustrating because he inherited some long-standing problems involving the need to increase funding and membership in the church and some more elusive problems having to do with demographic changes in our small town. As we struggled to find an effective working relationship on these problems, it became apparent that we needed to define the respective roles of the pastor and the board.

The process used to accomplish this has applications for many churches because it improves communication between pastor and lay leadership. Better communication is a primary need in a great many churches as our surveys of pastoral concerns have shown.

---

[1]This material (to the end of this chapter) was originally published as an article in the March-April, 1979, issue of *Your Church,* Religious Publishing Company, King of Prussia, Pennsylvania.

Developing a Job Description That Communicates

Defining the pastor's job is not inherently difficult, but simply drawing up a list of duties is just a beginning. Making the list starts the process of breaking down misconceptions of what is expected of the pastor. Expressing the duties in terms the pastor and the leadership understand in the same way begins that process.

How do you go about it? This is one simple but effective approach:

1. Lay leaders and the pastor agree on the desirability of developing a job description and on some simple ground rules for its format and content. (The lay leaders may be represented by a personnel committee or some other unit of the lay leadership. The process is unduly complicated if it involves the entire board at each step.)
2. The lay leaders draft a description embodying their perspective on the pastor's job.
3. At the same time, but independently, the pastor drafts his or her own description.
4. Pastor and leadership exchange drafts, then meet to discuss and reconcile differences.

The purpose of step 4 is to highlight not only the differences in viewpoints but also the reasons for the differences. Reconciling conflicts may not be easy, but not facing them is worse by far.

What emerges from the meeting is not only a document but also a clearing of the air between pastor and board. They have talked their way through the church's overall program and its various administrative activities to determine the pastor's responsibilities in each area. This discussion will also involve exploring the responsibilities of the various church committees in the same areas.

Problems that cannot be specifically resolved in that meeting are noted, and plans are made for settling those differences within the appropriate committees.

This process results in a written job description. An example is shown as Exhibit 1-1, found at the end of this chapter. Note that the format identifies areas of responsibility rather than listing duties or procedures. The "how to" is left up to the pastor as a trained professional. This format minimizes nit-picking and endless discussions over wording.

Setting Standards of Performance

Now let's move to the second component, setting standards of performance for the pastor's job. Here again some pastors will say, "Lay people are not in a position to set standards for me and my work." They may have a point, but an exchange of views on what lay people expect and what the pastor intends in the way of results from his or her work is vital to their continuing relationship. This is just as important as the job description.

The process of developing standards can follow this sequence:

1. In the meeting in which the two job descriptions are exchanged discuss the standards desired, taking up each area of responsibility and its standard individually. This discussion is aimed at mutual understanding of what standards of performance are, how they are to be used (as discussed later in this chapter), and at finding ways of expressing standards for two or three areas of responsibility. Nothing should be written down at this stage. What you want to achieve is a mutual understanding of what a standard of performance is and how it can be expressed.

2. The pastor and leadership retire to develop their respective versions of standards of performance, one for each area of responsibility of the pastor.

3. At the same time both pastor and leadership agree to prepare statements on the responsibilities of the lay leadership in helping the pastor carry out his or her role as expressed in the job description. This assignment will alert both parties to an awareness that the pastor cannot be expected to perform his or her role in a vacuum, that there is a team relationship that needs to be enunciated.

4. Then the pastor and leaders meet to review, explore differences, and formulate mutually agreeable written statements of standards.

Exhibit 1-1 is an example of a job description, standards of performance, and leadership responsibility statements. The reader may disagree with the manner of expression, degree of specificity, or other elements in this sample. Keep in mind that the real benefit lies in the process of discussion, in identifying and reconciling differences in perspective. The real benefit is in the communications—the document is a means to this end.

A further value of the job description is in hiring a new pastor. The lay board may choose to modify the existing description to reflect changed perceptions about the pastor's role. The job description serves as a useful basis for agreeing upon what is expected of candidates for the job.

Appraising Job Performance

Finally there is the issue of actually measuring or appraising the pastor's performance. This must be an acknowledged purpose of the whole process right from the start. Both parties must agree at the outset that achievement of this purpose is desirable if it can be accomplished in a fair, unemotional, and logical manner.

The basic tools of the appraisal are the job description, standards of performance, and statement of lay responsibility. The appraisal process can follow this sequence:

1. Pastor and leadership prepare for a meeting by independently making notes on the extent to which each standard of performance has been met during the prior period. The "prior period" would usually be the year just passed, but in the case of a new minister appraisals might be done at six-month intervals until the major "settling in" issues are resolved.
2. The preparation should also include suggestions for any revisions to the job description, standards, or statement of lay responsibilities to the pastor.
3. Both parties meet to discuss their respective notes in a frank, informal way. The focus should be on the pastor's activities and results. *Salary should not be one of the topics at this discussion.* Any discussion of salary and benefits should be saved for another meeting, preferably separated from this discussion by several months.

The main purposes of this discussion are:

1. Communication of mutual expectations and perceptions of results.
2. Discussion of what can be done to make more progress in the affairs of the church as they pertain to the team relationship of the pastor and leadership.
3. Illumination of what the leadership can do to help the pastor—in self-development, in providing resources, and in dealing with problems.

This appraisal process also provides the basis for identifying changes in the leadership's expectations of the pastor. As the church grows, as programs change, and as priorities shift, these changes can be reflected in revised standards of performance. When performance standards are used, the potential for conflict between the pastor and the lay board is minimized.

The main benefits of adopting this approach accrue to the pastor. I know from many discussions with pastors on church management that communication with lay leadership—in terms the laity can understand and the pastor can accept—is vital. This approach to pastoral performance appraisal stimulates that communication in a realistic, factual, and supportive manner.

Considerable improvement in the working relationship and job results has been evident in organizations where the appraisal process has been properly introduced and applied by both parties. The same kind of improvement is possible in the church situation, where the traditional barriers to communication are greater. These barriers can be overcome by thoughtful discussion of these concepts and agreement to make them work.

Exhibit 1-1   Job Description

Note: Under each duty statement is a "standard of performance," provided to assist in planning the work and in evaluating the pastor's performance.

Overall purpose of this position

To lead the spiritual development of the congregation and foster its commitment to Jesus Christ as described in the Word of God; to guide and participate in methods to increase membership; and to guide and support religious, social, and administrative activities of the church.

DUTIES

Preaching and Teaching

1. Preach at regular worship services, and conduct special

services as needed (i.e., funerals, weddings, baptisms, Easter, Christmas, etc.)

The standard of performance is met when sermons reflect thoughtful preparation and when sermons and other aspects of services are presented in a manner which communicates effectively their significance as meaningful aspects of worship.

2. Organize and lead the church's youth program.

The standard is met when a meaningful youth program is generating active participation by our youth and contributes to leading them toward church commitment and participation in its activities.

3. Conduct classes for new communicants, including children and new adult members.

The standard is met when communicant classes are promptly scheduled as needed, and conducted with sound teaching practices on the doctrine and government of this denomination.

4. Act as resource for standing and special committees of the church; attend committee meetings as appropriate; serve as resource to Sunday school as needed.

The standard of performance is met when pastor is knowledgeable on the current effectiveness and needs of the committees; and when both guidance to the committees and follow-up for action are promptly provided as needed by committees.

Visitation and Counseling

5. Provide pastoral care to communicants of this church through regular visitation and other special needs, i.e., Communion to shut-ins, etc.; plan and carry out regular schedule of visitations to insure coverage of attending and nonattending communicants; be available for and provide counseling to those needing help.

The standard of performance is met when the pastor is knowledgeable on the current concerns of members of the congregation; is promptly following up for action where indicated and where appropriate to his role; and when counseling help is promptly available through the pastor and is provided by him or her in a useful manner.

6. Participate in planning visits to prospective members and visit these families to acquaint them with the church.

   The standard is met when the membership of this church is growing at a rate consistent with growth of the community (a suggested target for 1981-82 is —%) and when this growth reflects both addition of new members and retention of present members.

Other Duties

7. Participate as appropriate in such church-related activities as fellowship dinners, men's breakfasts, youth athletics, etc.

   The standard of performance is met when participation in these activities reflects the pastor's interest in and support of their purposes.

8. Participate as appropriate in community and professional activities (i.e., Community Ministerial Association, Crisis Control, community drives, etc.) as a means of representing the church to the community.

   The standard is met when church and its pastor are perceived as interested and concerned community participants.

9. Participate in committees, camps, and other duties as assigned by the denominational leadership.

   The standard is met when assigned duties are discharged in an efficient manner.

10. Carry out or direct administrative functions, such as those relating to the use and maintenance of the building and property, publishing church bulletin and newsletter, correspondence, files, inventories, etc.

    The standard is met when administrative functions are carried out on regular schedules and with effective delegation to volunteer staff where appropriate.

Self-Development

11. Set targets for self-development and engage in study, seminars, and other activities designed to assist in meeting these targets.

> The standard is met when the pastor and the officers have identified areas requiring self-improvement and when targets are being met consistently.

Evaluation of Pastor's Performance

Evaluation will take place not less than annually. Evaluation will be by an evaluation committee composed of:
1. Moderator or other designated lay leader
2. President of the women of the church
3. Chairperson of board of deacons or vice-moderator of the session

The role of this committee is to:
1. Seek evaluation input from all church organizations.
2. Prepare and conduct with the pastor the review of his or her performance against job standard; providing counsel to him or her in areas requiring improvement in present performance and in means of self-development.
3. Develop recommendation to the congregation regarding salary adjustment.

GUIDELINES

A. *Priorities and Time Allocation*

	Priorities
Preaching and Teaching—50 percent of work week	A
Visitation and Counseling—25 percent of work week	A
Other Duties—25 percent of work week	B

B. *Work Week*
1. The expected work week would normally be forty-two hours.
2. There is need for some regularity of schedule for the benefit of both the pastor and the members of the congregation.

3. The schedule of times the pastor will be in the church office will be published.

RESPONSIBILITIES OF OFFICERS

1. Set standards for measuring progress of church toward its goals and periodically evaluate progress.
2. Determine steps necessary to remedy problems in meeting goals and direct corrective action.
3. Evaluate performance of pastor in carrying out his or her duties and communicate to him or her on needs for improvement.
4. Provide necessary resources to pastor for carrying out his or her agreed-upon responsibilities.
5. Be knowledgeable on pastor's program for this church and work in partnership with pastor to overcome short- and long-term obstacles to achieving the program.

Chapter 2

Strategic Planning

Why plan? Why ask this question? Don't most people recognize the values of planning?

The answer, unfortunately, is "no." As a consultant, an executive introducing planning into a major corporation, and a leader of numerous seminars on planning, I concluded long ago that planning is not a "natural" activity for most people. These are some of the reasons:

1. It is human nature to think more about immediate concerns. Planning is something that can be put off until tomorrow.
2. Managing by planning usually involves a change in decision-making style. This change is hard for people to adopt.
3. Planning initially takes a fair amount of effort. Unless people can clearly see benefits accruing to them personally, they hesitate about putting in the effort.

Curiously, the reasons people give for not managing by planning are not the same as those I have just cited. Instead managers offer reasons such as these:

1. Nobody can predict the future—it's too fuzzy.
2. How can plans help you when you know things are going to change in the next few years?
3. We don't want to straightjacket our people with a lot of plans.

4. We know our organization and its problems so well that there's no need to get formal about planning.
5. We're too busy running the day-to-day activities to plan.

These are common excuses. None of them is really valid. They reflect a lack of understanding of what planning is all about. I hope in this chapter to be able to clarify some of those misconceptions.

The arguments *in favor of planning* are based on some very simple premises:

1. Every organization needs to do some systematic planning for its future. Otherwise the future will just "happen" without any preparation. Organizations do not achieve their goals without planning.
2. Communications is one of the greatest needs in any organization. Planning is one of the most effective means of communication there is. When key people in an organization are involved in assessing the future, setting targets, and evaluating ways of achieving those targets, the result is real communication.
3. Planning provides the rationale for allocation of an organization's resources to its various activities. Without planning these resources in all likelihood will not be used efficiently. No organization has limitless resources.
4. Planning provides the basis for measuring and controlling programs and individual efforts to ensure that these are directed toward the goals of the organization. In its simplest terms, this means getting maximum horsepower out of an organization and its people.

What Is the Planning Process?

Strategic planners recognize that no one can accurately predict the future. Planning is not forecasting. Rather, planning *is* making reasonable assumptions about what the future will be in order to make decisions today.

Planning provides a framework for making management decisions. This framework includes a base of pertinent information, logical goals, and a means of evaluating alternatives in order to select the best decisions for your church.

Let's look now at how the planning process accomplishes this. The planning process involves several sequential steps:

1. Analysis of the external environment.
2. Analysis of internal capabilities.
3. Determination of opportunities and threats, strengths and weaknesses, key issues.
4. Setting objectives.
5. Selecting strategies which enable you to achieve your objectives.
6. Developing action plans (tactics).
7. Determining the budget.

The last two steps listed, "developing action plans" and "determining the budget," are dealt with in other chapters. We will focus here on steps 1 through 5 which are the long-term (more than one year) aspects of planning.

How long is long-term planning? The common practice is to think in terms of five years. The first year is the period of the short-range (one year) plan; beyond five years, one moves into the area of "futures planning" (see Appendix, "Implications of the Future").

Analysis of the External Environment

Every church operates in its own external environment which includes the community, the state, the nation, the world, and its denomination. Within these micro- and macro-environments there is a wide mix of trends impacting on your church.

Let's suppose you are a member of your church's long-range planning committee; and the committee chairman asks the committee, as its first task, to identify and evaluate the external trends significant to your church and its future. What trends are your committee members likely to identify?

It is likely that your list will include such trends as these:

1. Economic trends in your locality, in your geographic region, and in the nation. Examples of these trends are changes in personal income, employment, land values, and industry location.
2. Demographic trends, including shifts in age groups, education levels, numbers of widows and retired people, and shifts of population to different geographic areas.
3. In your community, the issues of urban vs. suburban development, growth or decline of commercial activities, transportation facilities.

4. Also in your community, changes in the services offered to people. Who is offering them? Are services primarily shifting into governmental hands or private sponsorship? How effective are these services in meeting the needs of the community?

5. Trends in competition for your "prime time"—Sunday mornings and evenings and perhaps weekday evenings. What other things are going on that present you with competition for that time?

6. Church attendance trends in your community and region and the reasons for changes in these trends. What activities in churches are proving to be the most popular at this point in time?

7. Changes in social values. What do people in your community look on as being important? Is churchgoing an important value? (Evaluation in this area can lead into issues, such as the strength of family relationships, attitudes toward moral values, etc.).

This is not a comprehensive list, but it should initiate discussion within your committee. These items are typical of trends in the external environment. Some of them present opportunities; others represent threats to your church.

In making an analysis of the external environment, essentially you are looking for opportunities and threats in the *trends of change*. Having identified these trends, you need to make some judgments as to the rate of change and the direction of the trend (increasing, decreasing, holding steady).

A key question now arises—where do you get information on these trends? Looking back at the list, a little thought will disclose the more obvious sources. Banks and the chambers of commerce are storehouses of economic data. Builders, real estate people, and local business leaders keep current on land values, industry changes, and shifts in the demographics of the community. The city planning board and the local utility companies are excellent sources. The mayor's office, the regional office of HEW, and the pastor are knowledgeable on issues on community needs and availability of services.

Most churches have within their congregation people who have the kinds of information that the external analysis requires. The key to tapping information sources is to formulate the right questions.

That's the job of your long-range planning committee.

A word of caution is needed on this issue. Avoid collecting too much information at the outset. Formulate a limited number of realistic questions to collect information you believe is really pertinent to your church's forward thinking. Much more data than you can possibly use is available. Accumulating a mountain of data is a great way to build a wall against doing planning.

Analysis of Internal Capabilities

This is step 2 for your planning committee. The purpose is to evaluate the resources of your church in order to compare them with the opportunities and threats identified in the external environment. This comparison or "assessment" will be the basis for setting the objectives for the church. After all, you are not likely to seize an opportunity or counter a threat unless you have the resources required and have decided to use them for these purposes. Your planning committee needs to understand this basic point. If they understand this principle, they will go through these first two stages of analysis with greater enthusiasm and effectiveness.

All right, how do we do "analysis of internal capabilities"? The planning committee should first develop a checklist of the church's various "resources" that need to be evaluated. Let's look at a representative list of resources and some evaluative questions relating to these—

1. Financial resources of the church, including operating funds, special funds, income, and expenditures. What has been our performance over the last five years in adhering to budget limits? What is our ability to raise funds when needed?
2. Equipment and space. Is it adequate for present needs and for planning future needs? Is it in good operating condition? Is it costly to maintain or operate?
3. The demographics of our congregation. How many people do we have in each age group? What are the basic categories of jobs and income levels? What percentage of the congregation consists of retired people or widows?
4. Sociological profile of our church. Are we conservative or liberal? Are we community minded? Does our church collaborate with other community agencies and institutions? As a church, what are our primary interests and social values?

5. Power structure of the church. Who makes the decisions and by what process?
6. Church organization and management. Quality of staffing, lay leadership, personnel policies, financial and business management capabilities, organization structure.
7. Present programs. What are they? Is the leadership in each program effective? How much interest and support from the congregation does each program have?

The planning committee needs to develop its own checklist of internal resources and capabilities. Then it should make brief evaluative notes on each item, noting key facts which can later be used to decide whether the particular capability is a strength or weakness. For example, having an experienced and well-loved pastor is a strength; but if he is two years from retirement, we have a potential weakness. We may have excellent day-care facilities; but if they are not being used, they are not really a strength.

It is usually helpful to review the entire internal capabilities checklist once to see where more information may be needed; then develop the additional information before proceeding further with evaluation.

A common problem with this step in planning is failing to be *objective* about internal capabilities. That's why the need for developing facts is stressed. Facts tend to speak for themselves. Furthermore, some member of the planning committee is likely to say, "Let's not bother writing all this stuff down—we've all been in the church long enough to know what its internal capabilities are." In a group of four or five people you are going to get surprising discussions on what the real capabilities of the church are in a number of areas.

However, since you are dealing with an organization you know well, this step of analyzing internal capabilities is not a tedious or drawn-out effort. With skillful committee leadership the task can be done in one or, at the most, two sessions.

Assessing Internal Capabilities vs. External Environment

This is step 3 of the planning process. Visualize taping your list of external trends on the wall; then alongside of it tape your analysis of internal capabilities. Now compare one to the other to identify opportunities and threats, strengths and weaknesses.

A trend in the external environment is really an opportunity for your church only if you have the internal capability to exploit it. A threat to your church emanating from the external environment must be evaluated in the light of your resources for countering this threat.

Your internal capabilities are strengths if they permit you to exploit an opportunity or counter a threat in the external environment. They are weaknesses if they do not permit this positive action.

Let's look at some typical examples of strengths and weaknesses resulting from this assessment step. One such example might be a church's day-care program. This program, carefully developed over the last several years, is doing an excellent job of which the church is justifiably proud. From an "internal capabilities" standpoint this is viewed as a strength.

However, in the external environment we find that other churches have been responding to the same need for day-care centers. Furthermore, the Mini-Schools chain has moved into town and set up three centers. The market for day care is pretty well saturated; thus the need for our churches' day-care services is considerably reduced. A capability which was a strength is a strength no longer.

Another example: the church has a relatively new classroom wing as well as a fine parish hall for group meetings, banquets, etc. Usage of these facilities is, at the most, six or eight hours a week. These facilities are a strength if there is a need for them in order to service a desired purpose. Until that need is defined and the facilities are being used for that purpose, the facilities are not a strength.

Setting Objectives

Unfortunately, many organizations view planning as a two-stage process involving "Where do we want to go?" (setting objectives) and "How are we going to get there?" (strategies and action plans). They fail to recognize that objective setting is not the real starting point of planning.

As we have discussed earlier in this chapter, the planning process must start with analysis of the external environment and of the internal capabilities. Unless this sequence is followed, objectives are not only difficult to establish, but they are also likely to be quite unrealistic. They will not be grounded in pragmatic considerations of what *needs* to be done and what *can* be done. Setting objectives is step 4 in the planning process.

With this caution in mind, *what guidelines* are most helpful in this task of setting objectives?

Objectives can be short-term or they can be long-term. It is important to establish the time frame in the statement of the objective itself.

Furthermore, a good objective statement needs to have a built-in yardstick enabling the leadership of the organization to evaluate progress toward the objective. For example, it is better to say, "We will increase congregation membership by 25 percent over the next three years," than, "Our objective is a significant increase in membership." Even better might be this statement: "We will increase membership by 10-15 percent for each of the next three years." The latter provides a yardstick for evaluating performance annually.

Other criteria for judging whether objectives are well stated and meaningful include these:

1. Are the objectives understandable?
2. Are the objectives feasible? Will our congregation have confidence that we can, in fact, accomplish them?
3. Do these objectives challenge people to increase effort in a meaningful way? Are they *motivating* concepts?

What kind of objectives will a church want to set for itself? The church is likely to establish objectives in these topic areas:

1. Growth in membership and/or in the geographic area served.
2. Range of programs and/or services to be offered, improved, expanded, or initiated.
3. Financial resources.
4. Physical resources or facilities (modernization, upkeep, expansion).
5. Collaboration with the community or sectors thereof.
6. Governance of the church (for example, an objective to revise the governance method to a unicameral system).
7. Constituency—people to be served or involved (for example, an objective to shift the makeup of the congregation to more younger people or more ethnic groups).

These are simply the examples of areas in which churches

typically set objectives. Your own selections will be tailored to your church's situation. However, another caution: limit the number of objectives to perhaps ten or twelve. A significantly longer list usually embraces tasks rather than long-term objectives. (Exhibit 2-1 provides examples of objectives developed by a church in its strategic planning efforts.)

Exhibit 2-1   Objectives for Outreach and Program Development

1. To become a growing church attaining an annual rate of net growth of fifty members per year by 1983, increasing to one hundred members per year by 1985.

2. To commit 50 percent of incremental funds to an expanded level of outreach by 1983.

3. To create a community awareness of the Christian ministry of this church through establishing a major media program beginning in 1981.

4. To conduct an evangelistic outreach emphasis in the spring of 1981.

5. To conduct a continuing series of quarterly events beginning in 1981 designed to involve total church participation and community outreach.

6. To emphasize 1981 as a year for renewal of spiritual life development through all the programs of the church.

7. To expand opportunities for church retreat activities beginning in 1981.

8. To establish a transportation service with the purchase of a minibus or bus to be used in the varied programs and ministries of the church by 1982.

9. To establish an ad hoc group to work with the associate pastor to study needs of and develop a comprehensive program with single adults by December, 1981.

10. To expand the program of leadership recruitment and training to undergird the total ministry of the church in 1981.

11. To implement a year-round program of continuing stewardship education beginning in 1981.

12. To increase the church's support of the denominational mission program beginning in 1981 with an increase in that year of 10 percent of the total church budget receipts.

13. To increase the total financial support of missions to a level of $125,000 per year by 1985.

With this reference to long-term objectives, let's recognize another fact about objective setting. In a church that is just starting up the planning process, it may be better initially to set a limited number of short-term objectives and leave the longer-term ones for later. The rationale is simply that the likelihood of accomplishing a few short-term objectives is much greater. Once the church organization or several committees have met some practical short-term objectives, their enthusiasm for the utility of defined objectives rises significantly. They are then more willing to commit themselves to longer term and perhaps more challenging objectives.

A little later in this chapter, reference will be made to the task of measuring performance against objectives. Suffice it to say here that there must be some periodic measurement of performance; otherwise the objectives lose their motivational strength rather quickly.

Strategies

In the field of planning, the concept of strategies seems to be the most difficult one for the lay person to grasp. One of the problems is that of making a clear distinction between objectives and strategies. Theoretically this is quite simple—an objective is where you want to get to; a strategy is a broad course of action that will get you there. But what is an objective to you may be a strategy to me. For example, you may say that it is our strategy to reach our growth objective by adding more community services. I might say that it is our objective to add more community services, which is one of several ways by which we intend to grow. These controversies do arise—but they are not particularly important. Some organizations resolve the problem very simply by grouping objectives and strategies together under a common heading.

Let's look at some guidelines for identifying strategies. A definition goes something like this: "A strategy is a broad course of action selected among alternative courses of action for reaching long-term objectives and involves the allocation of resources in order to implement the strategy."

What does this say? "Broad course of action" means something that can encompass a variety of tactics. "Alternative courses of action" means that there are various ways to attain a long-term objective. For example, take an objective of growth. The strategic choices are by merger with another church, by promotion, or by adding services. Take an objective of improving financial resources. The strategic choices are increasing income, reducing costs, or both.

A key phrase is "allocation of resources." A strategy involves allocating a resource, such as money or people, to a basic course of action which will improve the condition of the church over time. If $10,000 is a major sum of money to your church, then spending it on one course of action would be a strategy. For another church $100,000 may be the "strategic" sum.

Selection of a desired strategy must be geared to the available or anticipated resources of the church, specifically people, funds, or facilities. Essentially the committee appraises which strategy will do the best job of ensuring attainment of the long-term objectives in the light of available resources.

Let's look at more examples of strategies illustrating ways in which a church can attain objectives. For example, let's assume that the objective is for growth expressed in some specific terms (i.e., double in five years). The strategy options might include these:

1. Grow by extension of more services needed by the community. Implementing this strategy may involve setting up program committees to plan and initiate specific services aimed at specific community segments requiring such services.

2. Adding capacity in order to respond to demand that has already been identified. This can be viewed as strategy since it involves the allocation of resources, namely, the major capital requirements of building facilities.

3. Training of the congregation in evangelistic methods. By so doing, the opportunities for adding membership are significantly increased. Of course, this strategy could also be employed to meet another objective, that of achieving greater parishioner involvement in the church.

Revising the Stategic Plan

In the preceding sections of this chapter we have outlined the basic concepts of strategic planning as they can be applied to a church. Strategic planning establishes the framework and direction of the church over the long pull. Once this framework has been established, it is normally necessary to make major revisions only when there is some really significant change in the external environment. An economic downtrend, for example, may change the timing of a building program. The movement of a new industry, with additional people, into a community may accelerate the rate of growth of the church membership.

These events, probably unforeseen at the time of the writing of the strategic plan, do not render the plan obsolete as some critics of planning are wont to charge. Rather, the existence of the strategic plan in writing greatly facilitates the church's ability to adjust to the new contingency or opportunity. The new development is appraised for its impact in specific terms on the church's strategic plan. Revisions are made in that documented plan to take account of the new developments. This is a much more systematic and logical way of dealing with the unforeseen than saying helplessly, "What do we do now?"

Short-Term or "Action" Planning

The action plan spells out the specifics of what we will do, who will do it, and when it will be done. An action plan normally is a one-year plan. It is much easier to develop than the long-term plan because it involves much less uncertainty. Most of us are not all that uncomfortable about looking a year ahead. After all, we are used to working out the budget for a year ahead. The action plan essentially is the logic that underlies the budget. Putting it another way, the budget is simply the financial expression of what it takes in dollars to carry out the one-year plan.

In chapter 3 the essential features of short-term planning are discussed in terms of developing individual church programs. The action plan, the church's one-year plan, is normally a summation of the several program plans.

Measuring Performance Against Objectives

Defined objectives represent commitments by the congregation and its leadership to certain accomplishments. Therefore, a key step in effective management-by-planning is periodic appraisal of progress toward long-term goals and achievement of short-term objectives.

In this appraisal step the value of clear, specific, measurable objectives becomes evident. When the "built-in yardsticks" are a part of the objectives statement, then measurement of accomplishment is greatly facilitated—i.e., percentage growth, reduction or containment of costs, numbers of participants in the program, etc.

The appraisal process should be done by the church leadership normally at the beginning of the annual planning cycle. Other appropriate times might be at the beginning of the stewardship campaign or as the first step in the budget revision process. Findings should, of course, be communicated to the congregation, taking this opportunity to stress the significance of the planning process to church management decisions.

Conclusions reached as a result of this appraisal against objectives become an input to the plan for the next year. They clarify the need for shifts in program targets, reallocation of resources, timing of efforts, even changes in organization.

How to Begin Strategic Planning

Strategic planning is not an easy process. For one thing, even business people on the lay board are not necessarily familiar with this process in their own businesses. Don't let that lack of knowledge stop you from pushing for strategic planning in your church. It simply isn't *that* difficult. Strategic planning involves common sense first and foremost.

However, it is important that the church leadership engaging in strategic planning talk through the concepts expressed in this chapter. They need to get themselves oriented to the idea that deciding "what we want to be like at some point down the road" is a useful activity. They must also come to accept the principle that managing the church in the context of a long-range plan, however simple, is preferable to managing it without any plan at all.

Second, don't try to "do it perfectly" the first time around. That's not possible and you shouldn't expect it. For the first time through the planning process your goal should be a limited one. A realistic goal for the first year of planning might be "Let's learn how to do this planning and find out where the rough spots are." Specifically you may decide to do something like this:

1. Go through all the steps in long- and short-range planning in a nine-month period from January to September (if September is when you start to finalize next year's budget).
2. In the process seek to learn what information is really important to your planning, what are the gaps in needed information, and what questions you really have to ask to decide where you're going to go and how you're going to get there.
3. Spend the next few months gathering the needed data.
4. In Year 2 concentrate just on refining objectives and strategies.
5. In Year 3 you should be in good shape to develop good sound basic planning. By this time your lay leadership will be pretty comfortable with the concepts and will be "over the hump" as far as developing basic information.

From that point forward, updating planning on a regular basis is not difficult. In fact, you will have saved so much time by avoiding the time-consuming efforts inherent in "management by crisis" that planning will seem pretty simple.

Looking back at the strategic planning process, you will perceive these values:

1. Strategic planning provides a framework within which short-term and program planning can be done in an organized, systematic manner.
2. Short-term objectives are made consistent with long-term objectives. This avoids a lot of the "backing up and starting over again" so typical of organizations that plan for the short term only.
3. Managing finances becomes a much more sensible, logical process. Money is now going to be spent on things that will enable you to reach defined, clear-cut goals. Money will be spent in a more "efficient" manner.
4. Commitment by both lay leadership and parishioners to the goals and philosophy of the church is greatly enhanced.
5. The effectiveness of your interaction with other organizations with whom you must coordinate efforts, including your own denomination, is greatly facilitated. When you are able to spell out for others your objectives and plans for achieving those objectives and the specific actions you'll be taking in

the short-term with the logic behind them, your ability to communicate with other organizations is increased. Furthermore, your ability to decide on your participation in their activities, in terms of whether this will further the progress of your church toward its objectives, is likewise increased.

Churches which are growing or declining in a period of change—and all churches fit into that category today—face perplexing choices among needs to fulfill and use of limited resources. Planning makes it easier to resolve these perplexing choices. "Knowing where you are going helps greatly in selecting the routes for getting there."[3]

[3]Anonymous.

Chapter 3

Annual Plans for Church Programs

The preceding chapter on "Strategic Planning" deals with the long-term perspective. The resultant strategic plan provides objectives, and strategies designed to achieve objectives, which are a framework within which the annual or short-term plans can be developed. The annual plans contain the specific action steps to be taken in the coming year which will represent progress toward the long-term objectives and in fulfillment of selected strategies.

The purposes of annual plans are to:

1. Establish targets to be met
2. Assign responsibilities
3. Determine timetables
4. Provide "measuring sticks" for evaluating progress
5. Communicate to all concerned the "what, how, when, why" of the effort being planned.

This chapter explores planning concepts pertinent to church programs or activity areas and focuses on how to plan for the short term (one year). Normally these programs are administered by permanent church committees (e.g., Sunday church school, day-care, stewardship, personnel). Each of these programs needs a plan of its own in order to be managed effectively.

The ideas in this chapter are based on the assumption that it is difficult to manage an organization effectively without a plan. In discussions with pastors and lay leaders this assertion is normally not challenged. Why, then, do so few churches develop systematic plans?

The answer is not hard to find. Many organizations don't plan because there is a considerable amount of hard work involved. The hardest part is getting started in planning. This is because, at the outset, a certain amount of new information needs to be gathered and classified. Also some hard questions on targets and priorities arise on which there may be considerable differences of opinion. In this chapter we will explore how these and other obstacles to planning can be overcome.

Some churches say "We have a plan," but upon examination this turns out to be the budget. A budget is a necessary *control* mechanism, but it is not the same as a plan. (Rather than engage in an argument with your church treasurer right at this point, let us go ahead and discuss an annual plan and see how it relates to a budget. The differences will then become apparent.)

Developing the One-Year Plan

The format of the plan is basically simple. It identifies the targets to be met and when they should be met. It specifies the "action steps" that will be taken to make progress toward the targets, who is responsible for these action steps, when action is required, and what resources are needed.

An approach that has been used with considerable success involves these steps:

1. A program committee, for example, nursery care, establishes a set of targets for the period ahead which it considers both challenging and practical of accomplishment.
2. This list of targets is circularized to both the governing lay board and to other program committees with which nursery care must interact, asking for informal feedback on possible conflicts.
3. The nursery care committee members then settle on their program targets, utilizing this input.
4. The committee members next complete the format of their operating plan. They decide *what* specific actions will be necessary in order to meet these targets. They agree on *who* will be responsible for taking the action steps. They decide *when* each of the action steps needs to be finished if the target

Exhibit 3-1 Example of Annual Plan (for a program)

Program: Nursery Care

Targets: 1. to meet nursery needs for all worship services
2. to staff program with adequate number of properly trained teachers
3. to provide equipment necessary for normal operating needs

	Action	Responsibility of:	When Action Is Needed	Resources Required
1.	Recruit four more teachers	Nursery Committee	by 6/1	—
2.	Develop and implement refresher training program	Nursery Committee	by 8/1	Purchase Manuals ($35)
3.	Refurbish nursery room	Ted Childs with Facilities Committee	by 3/15	Estimate: $850
4.	Plan for Wednesday evening nursery facility	Nursery Committee	by 8/1	Cleanup crew
5.	Rewrite procedure manual	Helen Simpson	by 7/1	—
	-etc.-			

schedules are to be met. If significant resources will be required, such as money, time of the pastor, voluntary help from the congregation, etc., these are noted. An example of format is shown in Exhibit 3-1. A basic principle in developing these documents is "Keep it simple!" These plans record the basic elements of the agreement.

5. The committee then evaluates the plan as to its *practicality*. Specifically these questions need to be asked: Are a few people responsible for too many tasks? Are we expecting too many things to be done at one peak time? Are we realistic in expecting the needed resources to be made available to us? This kind of hard, objective look at the plan, with resulting modifications where indicated, is important in making the planning process meaningful.

The plan document is then brought to the governing board along with plans for each of the other church programs (for an example of a plan format for a project see Exhibit 3-2). The governing board makes a cross-analysis of the individual plans to see how they fit together, asking such questions as:

1. Are the priorities for each program practical when related to the other programs?
2. Are the same resources of money, time, and people going to be required for more than one program?
3. Do the timetables for one program mesh logically with timetables for other related programs?
4. Are the targets for each of the programs consistent with the overall targets set by the church in its long-range planning?

This overall review may turn up issues requiring the review by the appropriate program committee. However, this process of "tightening up" the plans can be normally done informally without paperwork or intercommittee meetings.

Communicating Plans to Those Concerned

Let's review where we are in the planning process. At this point:

1. Each committee has developed targets for its program.
2. These targets have been reviewed with the governing board to assure that they are realistic and mesh with the overall long-term program of the church.

Exhibit 3-2   Example of a Plan for a Project

Goal: To establish a ministry to the growing segment of single adults in our city and to receive fifty such persons as new church members by year-end.

	Action	Responsibility of:	When Action Is Needed	Resources Required
1.	Develop data on numbers, location, ages, etc., of single adults	Chairperson, missions committee	1/15	
2.	Conduct preliminary survey of sample of single adults to assess problems in making contact	"	2/15	Pastor participation
3.	Develop plan for establishing this ministry, including short-term goals, strategy, and steps	Task force (assigned by chairperson), missions committee	3/30	
4.	Publicize plan via pastor's weekly radio message	Pastor	4/15	
5.	Conduct contact calling	Task force plus volunteers	4/16–7/1	eight to ten volunteers
6.	Assess progress; revise plan as needed	Chairperson, missions committee with task force	7/15	

3. The program committees have then developed action plans to achieve their targets.
4. Their action plans have been reviewed by the governing board to ensure necessary coordination *between* programs.

By following these steps, certain major communications benefits have already been achieved:

1. Communication among the members of each program committee on "where we're going," "how we will get there," and "who will do what, and when."
2. Communication between each committee and the governing board on a basis that ensures feedback in a specific, practical manner.

The next step is, then, to distribute each committee's plan to the other committees and to members of the church staff. Why should this be done?

A church is a relatively small organization. Communication can be simple but effective, provided it is "worked at." Plans are a superb method of communication between organization units. They are in writing; they follow a consistent format; they are developed to express clearly targets and methods of accomplishing targets. It is important that each program committee know what each other program committee is doing. Thus dissemination of all plans among all committees is highly desirable.

And, of course, there is the need for communicating with the congregation as a whole. Here again the plans serve as an excellent method of communicating to the congregation what is planned. An effective method is for the governing board to summarize and distribute a summary outline of targets and plans of action of the program committees.

Developing and Supporting the Budget

Now we are ready to finalize the budget. To illustrate why this step is placed last in the planning sequence, we need to examine the relationships between the budget and the plan. (This discussion on the budget is designed to show how the budget [as an element of financial management] is linked into the planning process. Chapter 4 on financial management examines the details of budget development and use.)

Our illustration is borrowed from increasingly common practice in well-run business enterprises. The planning process in these companies follows these basic steps:

1. In the early part of the year, for example, January to July, the business examines its external environment and internal capabilities and reassesses its long-range goals and strategies. The result of this process is usually an updated five-year plan following the basic concepts outlined in chapter 2 on strategic planning.

2. In the second half of the year, management works on the "one-year business plan" which incorporates essentially the same concepts we have been discussing in this chapter. The one-year plan with its targets and action steps is approved, say, about the middle of November.

3. At that point the plan is turned over to the budget department to finalize budget numbers reflecting anticipated revenues and expenditures for the coming year (the year covered by the one-year plan). Since the budget people have actually been working closely with the department heads during the process of developing the one-year plan, the stage of "finalizing the budget" is not complex. It involves essentially:

   1. tightening the estimates of monthly revenue and expenses;
   2. putting them into a budget format;
   3. determining if there is adequate revenue to cover costs;
   4. checking back with the department heads to adjust plans either to increase revenues or reduce costs;
   5. bringing the budget in balance.

In the typical church budgeting process the starting point is usually an estimate of anticipated revenues. Then the amounts allocated to programs are adjusted to fit the anticipated revenue total. In the planning and budgeting process described previously, the emphasis is placed on first determining what results are desired and what actions are necessary to accomplish those results. Then the cost is determined program by program. The budget that emerges as the final step in this process is one geared to planned goals and activities. The budget is the *result* rather than an end in itself.

"But," some businesspeople on the budget committee will ask, "what if the expenditures portion of the budget (arrived at by this process) is significantly greater than anticipated revenues?" To answer this, let's turn to the issue of bringing revenues in line with planned expenditures.

Your church may use one of several methods for generating revenues from the congregation. It is not our purpose to go into specific techniques for this. Let us, rather, make a conventional assumption—that you conduct a two-month stewardship campaign in the fall. The pledges secured in this campaign represent anticipated, and thus budget, revenues.

What are some basic motivations of parishioners in response to your request for their financial pledge?

1. People like to know *what* their money is going to be spent for.
2. They want to know that their money given is not going to be wasted, meaning that some *desirable results* will be achieved by the expenditures.
3. They like to have confidence that the church's *financial affairs are well managed*.
4. They prefer to have *some input* into the decision process as to how much money will be raised and why (this statement may not be entirely valid; people often don't offer any ideas when asked for them).

The planning process discussed in this chapter provides a systematic means of satisfying all of these needs. Experience has shown that it is highly desirable to get reaction from the congregation on the one-year plan *before* initiating the stewardship campaign. Therefore, the attention of the congregation is focused on *what* is to be done rather than the *cost* of doing it.

For a church particularly this focus is highly desirable because it leads to a broader view of the opportunities available for growth and service. Of course, issues of "what will it cost?" will come up and should be answered in discussions of the plan. But at this point good ideas are encouraged even though they represent additional expenditures.

By engaging the congregation in a dialogue on objectives and action programs, it is possible to gain their endorsement of the programs for the year ahead without bogging down into debates on matching revenues and expenditures which are best handled in the budget committee anyway.

It follows that when the stewardship campaign is initiated, it is presented in terms of raising sufficient funds to carry out the plan already adopted. This justification or rationale for pledging is far more understandable and acceptable to the average parishioner than the more typical plea of "give at least what you gave last year and more if you can."

The budget committee may well want to go through the arithmetic of determining total planned expenditures and dividing by active members of the congregation to arrive at an estimated average pledge required. Or they may choose to present the pledge issue in terms of percentage of income. Whatever the guidelines for amount of individual pledge, the key point is that some finite relationship between the plan and the need for funds needs to be developed.[1]

Responsibility for Planning

Responsibility for putting these ideas into practice should normally be assumed by an existing committee or board. Introducing planning is the responsibility of the top management of an organization—in a church, the pastor and the governing lay board. They may choose to use the budget committee and convert it into a "planning and budgeting committee" to carry out details of the process. But overall responsibility for planning the future course of the church cannot be delegated. The process has to be managed from the top.

Since the main purpose of planning is to secure commitment to take action to achieve desired results, it is highly important to see that the results are being achieved. This is the responsibility of the pastor and the governing board.

First, as discussed earlier, the objectives or goals should be stated in such a way that progress toward them can be measured (see discussion on objectives in chapter 2).

Each committee is responsible for measuring its own progress and taking necessary action to stay on planned schedules.

The governing board may request of each committee a quarterly report of progress toward objectives. This could be as informal as a verbal communication, or it could be a brief written report. But the report should be in terms of the planned targets and actions with an

[1] The discussion above draws on established concepts of planning and budgeting as practiced in many well-run business organizations. Many of the same basic ideas are incorporated in N. C. Murphy, *Commitment Plan Handbook* (1973).

accompanying statement of expenditures. The practice of church committees reporting on the status of their programs regularly during the year is, of course, not at all unusual. The difference under the planning concept is that the reporting is "against plan."

On an annual basis there should be a thoughtful examination of each major program in enough detail to assess its effectiveness. Questions which should be asked are: Do members of the congregation still want this program? Is the program meeting its objectives? If not, are the objectives appropriate? What are the costs of the program in terms of resources which could be released to other and perhaps more worthwhile programs if this program were terminated? Should more resources be committed to improve the program? For a particular program or activity additional and more specific questions might be asked.

Although the type of evaluation can be conducted at any time, it makes sense to conduct it at a natural break or during a slack period. This probably means holding the evaluation sometime during the summer months, preferably at the beginning of the summer when recently completed programs are still clear in people's minds. One final consideration to be made when conducting an evaluation of a program is that every person responsible for making decisions pertaining to the program should be involved in the evaluation process.

Is Planning Worthwhile?

Planning is a year-round process, as has been noted at several points in this and other chapters. Sometimes this degree of planning activity strikes committees as being "planning for planning's sake" rather than emphasis on "getting the work done." Help them to recall that this process includes these elements:

1. Targets are set to determine what results are desired.
2. Program activity is organized to meet the targets within the financial constraints established by the budget.
3. During the year plans are implemented.
4. During a period of perhaps two months in the latter part of the year accomplishments are reviewed and goals are set for the year ahead.

Does this approach to managing the affairs of the church warrant the time and effort required? Once people get used to managing in this way, it's actually easier because they have a much clearer idea where they're going and how to get there.

Such planning permits church leaders to increase understanding and commitment significantly on the part of volunteer and paid staff and the congregation as a whole. It provides a basis for substantially enhancing mutual support for the goals and programs of the church. It provides a rationale for fund raising. It simplifies problem solving.

Is planning worthwhile?

Chapter 4

Annual Financial Management

This chapter is about preparing and working with the church's annual financial plan. We begin by considering the philosophy of financial management with primary attention being given to basic principles of planning and control. In addition, benefits and possible pitfalls are considered. Next we go through the procedure of constructing a budget—the most essential component of the annual financial plan. Then financial control is examined. Finally we discuss briefly the application of minicomputers to the preparation of church financial statements.

A question which frequently concerns a pastor is: "What should be my role with respect to the financial management of my church?" In most churches it is inappropriate for the pastor to be involved with the details of preparing financial statements. Nevertheless, he or she should fully understand financial documents and their construction. The pastor should also be involved in the decision as to the general types of financial statements to be used if not the exact details to be included in each statement. Most important, *it is the pastor's responsibility to ensure continuity in the financial planning process from one year to the next.*

Given this statement of the pastor's role, the chapter has four purposes:

1. It presents helpful principles of financial planning and control, particularly for the pastor who is relatively unsophisticated in financial management.

2. It introduces the concept of what we call a "programs/functions" budget, which is a budget showing full allocation of all expenses to the church's primary programs.
3. It provides examples of a number of useful financial statements which might serve as models for your church.
4. It demonstrates some simple but effective techniques to achieve financial control.

The annual canvass is given only limited coverage here since its role is discussed in chapter 3 and since most denominational offices provide extensive canvass-planning materials. The approach taken in this chapter does assume congregational pledging and annual canvass, however.

The procedures described in this chapter are oriented to the financial management needs of the medium-sized church (a congregation of, say, five hundred to seven hundred members). However, the basic principles presented are equally appropriate for smaller or larger churches. The procedures can be modified readily to meet particular needs without sacrificing the benefits.

Philosophy of Financial Management

In simple terms, financial management is determining what financial needs must be met in the current year, identifying sources of funds to meet those needs, establishing a procedure to raise the money, making adjustments in spending and/or fund-raising plans if anticipated income does not match financial needs, and maintaining control over income and expenditures. In essence, sound financial management is just good stewardship.

Let's look at several corollary definitions. *Financial planning* is deciding on the financial steps the organization intends to take during some specified period in the future, choosing someone to take them, and deciding when they'll be taken. *Control,* the natural complement of planning, involves ensuring that the steps are taken by the individual specified in the plan when they're supposed to be taken and that desired results are achieved. Planning gets the financial train moving; control keeps it on the track, headed in the right direction, and on time.

Benefits of Financial Management

Good financial management has several benefits. First, it permits the church to take a simpler, more reasoned, and more orderly approach to its affairs. A basic principle of management is that repetitive activities with predictable outcomes should be routinized as much as possible so that managment time can be reserved for dealing with problems which are neither routine nor predictable. Simplifying financial management means that the substantial effort frequently and unnecessarily devoted to financial matters can be channeled into more productive tasks.

Second, good financial management allows the church to anticipate and adjust to changes in local economic conditions. An economic downturn is always an unhappy event, but much of its unpleasantness can be avoided if financial management principles are employed.

Third, wise financial management contributes to the successful conduct of the annual stewardship campaign because financial planning focuses attention on the church's financial needs and on the resources available to meet them.

Annual Financial Management Principles

Let's examine some basic principles which should undergird your church's financial management program.

Simplicity of Documentation. Church financial planning documents should be simple and straightforward. Simple documents require less time for preparation (time is always an important consideration when volunteers are involved), and they are easier for church leaders without formal financial training or experience to follow.

Timeliness. Obviously timeliness is an important consideration when money must be raised, bills must be paid, and church employees must know what their salaries will be in the coming year. Timeliness is also of major importance when a church's financial planning and control system is a component of an overall planning and control system. If a single component of the total system is badly out of sequence, the whole system can easily become a useless and costly burden.

Systematization. Good financial management is systematic. It emphasizes minimization of effort and standardization of procedures. It permits leaders to focus on nonroutine issues and not on procedural revisions. It is the pastor's job to ensure that the financial management system is not "reinvented" each time a new lay financial officer is appointed. A basic set of procedures should be designed and implemented for the long run. Of course, details will change as conditions change, but basic procedures should not vary from year to year.

Congregational Orientation. A financial management system should be oriented to the needs of its users. On the input side it is important to push responsibility for developing financial information down to the lowest possible level. On the output side it is equally important to ensure that financial data is available to everyone in the congregation. However, inundating people with numbers doesn't mean a financial management system is user-oriented—congregational orientation implies only that the system should provide as much information as people find useful but no more.

Consistency of Format. Financial statements with consistent formats are easier to produce, read, and interpret. Consistency of format contributes to maintaining continuity of approach from governing board to governing board and makes it easier for old board members to step back into harness after being away from the board for several years. Format standardization also facilitates computerization of the financial planning and control system when the time is ripe to do so.

Responsibility. Normally one individual should be assigned responsibility for financial management (although ultimate responsibility still rests with the pastor and the governing board). Usually the individual responsible would be either the church treasurer, the chairperson of the finance committee, or the budget director reporting directly to the chairperson. Because of the need for close coordination of financial activities, the pastor, the church treasurer, the canvass director, and the church's principal financial officer should all be members of the finance committee.

Annual Financial Plan—The Budget

The annual budget is the church's most important financial planning tool. Like a handy household tool the budget should be employed frequently. If the budget isn't used much, something is wrong. In the early stages of the annual financial management process the budget is a planning document indicating how much money will be spent in the coming year and how it should be allocated. As a church gets ready for a new fiscal year, the budget becomes a promotional vehicle focusing attention on the funding needs of church programs and activities. During the church's fiscal year, however, the budget is primarily a control vehicle. It spotlights areas in which the financial plan is not being achieved, and it provides some clues as to where remedial action should be taken.

The "Programs/Functions" Budget Concept

We define "programs" to be major categories of services a church provides to one or more of the identifiable groups with which it interacts. Examples of programs are: worship, Christian education, and outreach. The term "activity" refers to a single component of a program. For example, within the worship program music might be one activity; preaching might be another. Or worship might be categorized by time and day of service, for example, 8:30, 11:30, or Vespers. Within the Christian education program, preschool education might be one activity, and adult education might be another. "Functions," on the other hand, refers to use of funds (and perhaps other resources) for purposes not keyed to a particular program, such as personnel expense, debt service, or utilities.

In most church budgets functional items account for a much larger share of expenditure than do programs. This situation results in the often-heard criticism that "most of our money goes to personnel and 'brick and mortar' instead of programs." This criticism is not only unfair, but it is also fallacious, the fallacy lying in the critics' failure to understand that personnel and facilities are every bit as essential to most church programs as is direct funding.

To deal with this misconception, the budget should be set up not as a mix between functional and program designations but as two separate budget "sections." One section is organized along program lines with a summary functional breakdown; the other is organized along strictly functional lines. Exhibit 4-4 is an example of the programs section of a programs/functions budget. Exhibit 4-5 is a simplified example of the functions section. (Each of the exhibits is explained in detail in the subsection "Constructing the Budget.")

When a church uses this budget format, all expenditures are ultimately allocated to programs. Therefore the governing board and congregation can determine if programs are overfunded or underfunded relative to congregational desires. At the same time the summary breakdown of functional expenditures for each major program indicates the amounts and types of resources supporting the major programs. This information is helpful to parishioners who are interested in seeing the relative levels of support for programs but not in seeing the financial "nuts and bolts." On the other hand, decision makers who require financial detail find it in the functions section of the budget. There specific items of expenditure, year-to-year comparisons, and trends would be provided on each of the functional breakdowns.

At this point an obvious question is: How are allocations of functional expenses made to programs? There are no easy answers to this question, but methods which should provide satisfactory results are available. For instance, personnel expense can be allocated to programs on the basis of the proportion of time a given staff member devotes to a program (a time log is useful for this purpose). Building charges can be allocated on the basis of the amount of time buildings are used to house specific programs. Equipment costs can be allocated using a similar approach. The rule is: Select whatever method makes sense and provides satisfactory results for your own church.

Constructing the Budget

A preliminary budget should be constructed about three months prior to the beginning of a new fiscal year (in most cases the church's fiscal year is the same as its calendar year). This much lead time is necessary to enable the budget director to secure needed information from staff and committee chairpersons, to conduct reviews and analyses, and to promote the budget to the congregation.

Exhibit 4-1 shows a simple timetable which has been found to be a useful way of keeping on schedule during the budget construction process. A more detailed timetable might be needed by the larger church. Let's examine each of the budget preparation steps outlined in the exhibit.

1. *Assigning Responsibility for Line Items*. Line items are specific activities or functions generating revenues or requiring expenditures. Exhibit 4-5 provides examples.

For purposes of control and accountability, responsibility for each line item in the budget should be assigned to one individual. Obviously one person can be responsible for several line items. Because church activities wax and wane in popularity and because individuals resign from committees and chairmanships, line item responsibility may be undefined from time to time. A good time to reassign unassigned responsibilities is early in the budget-setting process.

2. *Distribute Budget Allocation Request Forms to Responsible Individuals.* Once line items have been assigned, budget allocation request forms should be sent to each individual responsible for submitting a request. Examples of two simple forms designed by the author are included as Exhibits 4-2 and 4-3.

The form illustrated in Exhibit 4-2 would be completed by individuals responsible for directing specific activities or programs, for example, the youth choir. Notice that the form in Exhibit 4-2 includes requests for program objectives, for a general plan of action, and for resource needs. When the planning process discussed in chapter 3 is being followed, this information is readily available and can simply be referenced on the form.

Exhibit 4-1 Budget Preparation Timetable*

	Task	Tentative Date of Completion
1.	Assign responsibility for line items if assignment has not been previously made.	9/1
2.	Distribute budget allocation request forms to individuals responsible for line items.	9/1
3.	Remind individuals responsible to return budget allocation request forms.	9/15
4.	Finance committee review of line item requests.	9/25
5.	Construct preliminary budget.	9/25
6.	Congregational program and budget review.	10/1
7.	Board review of preliminary budget.	10/10
8.	Implement the canvass plan.	10/10
9.	Begin canvass.	10/15
10.	Conclude canvass.	11/5
11.	Construct *pro forma* income statement.	11/5
12.	Board review of *pro forma* income statement.	11/10
13.	Construction of actual budget.	11/15

*Assumes fiscal and calendar years are the same.

Exhibit 4-2   Budget Request Form A

Program Subplan and Request for Allocation of Resources

Name of Program: _____

Program Objectives: _____

_____

_____

_____

General Plan of Action (activities, date, responsible persons, etc.)

_____

_____

_____

_____

_____

_____

_____

_____

Space Needs (rooms, number of tables, number of chairs, any special parts of the buildings): _____

_____

_____

Equipment Needs:

Movie Projector ( ) Screen ( ) Carousel Slide Projector ( )
Tape Recorder ( ) Mimeograph ( ) Craft Materials ( )
Storage ( )   Other _____

_____

_____

Necessary Program Costs (the funds you *have* to have):

Description	*Amount*
_____	_____
_____	_____
_____	_____
_____	_____
_____	_____

Exhibit 4-2 (continued)

Discretionary Program Costs (what you would like to do if you had the money):

Description	Amount	Rank
_____	_____	_____
_____	_____	_____
_____	_____	_____
_____	_____	_____
_____	_____	_____

Projected Cash Needs by Month:

Jan. Feb. Mar. Apr. May June July Aug. Sept. Oct. Nov. Dec.
___ ___ ___ ___ ___ ___ ___ ___ ___ ___ ___ ___

Requested by: _____ Date _____

The necessary and discretionary cost estimates and projection of expected cash needs (cash flow) by month are employed in the budget-setting process. With this form virtually all the information needed for planning and budgeting is collected at one time. The form has several other advantages:

1. It forces an activity director to think hard about plans for the coming year and about how tasks will be accomplished.
2. It is a useful guide to a successor should an activity director resign unexpectedly, thus enhancing program continuity.
3. It puts an activity or program director on record. A written statement of objectives is an important motivator in any volunteer organization.
4. Information contained in the request form, especially statements of necessary and discretionary program costs, is very helpful to the church's governing board if the preliminary budget exceeds income expectations.
5. Cash flow projections provide information for financial control, for cash management, and for short-term investment decision making.

6. When line item requests are segregated into necessary and discretionary components, the "discretionary expenditures" section may fire the imagination of the activity director completing the form.

The sample form in Exhibit 4-3, "Request for Allocation of Resources," would be sent to an individual responsible for a functional line item, such as the pastor's housing allowance or building maintenance and repair. In many instances little explanation would be required when an increase in funding is requested (consider, for example, a requested increase in utilities allowance to keep up with inflation). In other situations, detailed explanation or reference to the pertinent short-term plan would be appropriate (building maintenance would be a good example here). Like the activities budget request form (Exhibit 4-2), this functional request form can serve as a guide to successors and to the governing board should budget paring be required. Notice that this form also requires the individual responsible to prepare a cash flow projection.

3. *Remind Individuals Responsible to Return Budget Allocation Request Forms*. All of us need reminders now and then—even pillars of the church. It's important to keep the planning process on schedule, and a gentle reminder shouldn't offend anyone.

4. *Finance Committee Review of Line Item Requests*. It is important that finance committee members review budget requests prior to assembling the preliminary budget. There are several reasons for this:

1. The review familiarizes all committee members with the justifications given for individual budget requests should the need for adjustments to the budget arise later.
2. Errors in the preparation of request forms are more easily detected when several people are involved in the checking process.
3. The canvass director (a member of the finance committee) obtains the next best thing to a personal request for funds from every individual submitting a line item to the budget. A canvass director who knows why funds are needed is likely to do a better job of raising them. Here it should be emphasized that close coordination between the budget director and the

Exhibit 4-3—Budget Request Form B

Request for Allocation of Resources

Budget line item _____

Current year funding request _____

Prior year funding _____

Explanation of any difference between current and prior year's
figures _____
_____
_____
_____
_____
_____
_____
_____

Expected Cash Needs by Month:

Jan. Feb. Mar. Apr. May June July Aug. Sept. Oct. Nov. Dec.
___ ___ ___ ___ ___ ___ ___ ___ ___ ___ ___ ___

Requested by: _____   Date _____

canvass director is bound to produce both a more successful
canvass and a sounder budget. The likelihood of interaction
between budget and canvass director is greatest when both
are members of the church's finance committee and when
coordination between the two is a stated financial policy
requirement.

5. *Construct the Preliminary Budget.* This is basically an
adding-up procedure in which the finance committee chairperson or
budget director aligns expenditure requests according to the
church's standard budget format and adds up the amounts, line item

by line item, to obtain program and function subtotals and, finally, a
total budget. All necessary and discretionary planned expenditures
are included, and no cuts are made at this point. Exhibit 4-4 is an
example of two components of the programs section of a proposed
programs/functions budget. Exhibit 4-5 is an example of the
functions section of the same budget. Some discussion of these two
exhibits is in order.

In the interest of brevity only two components of the programs
section of the proposed budget are represented: missions and
worship. Depending on the individual church's definitions of
programs, the programs budget may embrace any number of
components (however, in the interest of maintaining simplicity,
there shouldn't be more than ten or twelve). Notice that each
program has associated with it a breakdown by activities and by
functions. Also notice that Exhibit 4-4 shows current year actual
figures, the proposed figures for the coming year, and percentages
of the total budget. Including actual and proposed figures enables
the individual examining the budget to make a number of useful
comparisons quite easily.

Exhibit 4-4 is complex and needs to be explained. (Since the
Missions and Worship components of Exhibit 4 are structurally
identical, only the Missions component is described.)

Columns labeled "Percent of Functional Allocation" in the top
half of Exhibit 4-4 (the Activities section) show how functional
expenditures are allocated to activities. For example, 5 percent of
the total amounts budgeted for personnel, facilities, equipment,
supplies/postage, and miscellaneous are allocated to the Cooperative program. Similarly, 58 percent of gifts and grants and 10
percent of books and periodicals are allocated to this activity.
Notice that none of the training budget was allocated. Using the
actual numbers, $.05(6,055) + .05(2,515) + .05(507) + .05(944) +
.58(15,435) + .10(139) + .05(214) = 9,478$ is the total allocation to
the Cooperative program in the current year. In the coming year,
the allocation is $.05(7,425) + .05(2,650) + .05(700) + .05(990) +
.55(16,781) + .10(120) + .05(220) = 9,841$. Notice that the current
and coming year totals are the same ($25,909 and $29,186) for both
the Activities and Functions sections of Exhibit 4.

The "Percent of Total Functional Expense" block in the
Functions section of the exhibit is a percentage breakdown of
expenditures by function in the program area. For example, of the

total amount of $25,909 allocated to Missions in the current year, 23 percent is personnel cost, 60 percent is gifts and grants, and so forth. The numbers on the diagonal should equal 100.

Although the detail shown in Exhibit 4-4 appears to be confusing and costly to produce, it is confusing only in its novelty. Judicious use of copying equipment can reduce production costs substantially for budgets produced after the original model is constructed. The church fortunate enough to have electronic word processing equipment can easily update documents used in prior years.

When this type of financial statement has been used once or twice, its basic simplicity becomes apparent. The numerical arrangement in Exhibit 4-4 shows at a glance how support funds are allocated to programs and activities. Church leaders can quickly see, by program, the volume and type of resource use. Without this kind of detail it is frequently impossible to determine which activities and programs are expensive and which are not. Budgets constructed according to this format are powerful tools enabling church leaders to make more rational resource employment decisions.

Exhibit 4-5 is a simplified example of the functions section of a programs/functions budget. The exhibit omits much of the detail that would actually be included in this section for a church of the size indicated by the numbers in the sample budget. Notice that the exhibit shows amounts for each line item for the current and coming years. It also shows percentages of the total budget accounted for by each major function. The programs section of the budget is designed as a control vehicle for use by all church leaders. The functions section, however, is more appropriate as a planning tool for the pastor, the business manager (if the church has one), and lay leaders responsible for financial matters.

6. *Congregational Program and Budget Review.* This meeting is held to inform the congregation about the proposed budget and to gauge feelings about the way program and activity chairmen and chairwomen plan to use their gifts to God. The review also begins the educational process so crucial to the success of the canvass. Based on the views expressed by members present, changes in the budget may be required. In the interest of avoiding an excessive number of congregational meetings, the budget review should probably be conducted when the one-year plan is presented (see chapter 3).

Exhibit 4-4—Missions and Worship Components of the Programs Section of a Programs/Functions Budget

Program: Missions

Activities	Current Year	(1)	(2)	(3)	(4)	(5)	(6)	(7)	(8)	Coming Year	(1)	(2)	(3)	(4)	(5)	(6)	(7)	(8)
		Percent of Functional Allocation									Percent of Functional Allocation							
Cooperative Program	9,478	5	5	5	5	58	100	10	5	9,841	5	5	5	5	55	100	10	5
World Mission	1,312	10	5	5	5	3	—	25	5	1,504	10	5	5	5	3	—	25	5
Local Mission																		
Contact	5,198	30	25	10	50	13		50	25	6,387	30	25	10	50	15		50	25
People in Need	4,138	20	25	15	15	13	—	15	25	4,488	20	25	15	15	12	—	15	25
Hospital House	4,437	30	25	50	15	10	—	—	25	5,457	30	25	50	15	12	—	—	25
Benevolences	1,346	5	15	15	10	3	—	—	15	1,509	5	15	15	10	3	—	—	15
Total	25,909									29,186								

Functions	Current Year	(1)	(2)	(3)	(4)	(5)	(6)	(7)	(8)	Coming Year	(1)	(2)	(3)	(4)	(5)	(6)	(7)	(8)
		Percent of Total Functional Expense									Percent of Total Functional Expense							
1. Personnel	6,055	23								7,425	25							
2. Facilities	2,515		10							2,650		9						
3. Equipment	507			2						700			2					
4. Supplies/Postage	944				4					990				4				
5. Gifts & Grants	15,435					60				16,781					58			
6. Training	100						—			300						1		
7. Books & Periodicals	139							—		120							—	
8. Miscellaneous	214								1	220								1
Total	25,909									29,186								
% of Total Budget	16.37									16.97								

Program: Worship

Activities

Activities	Current Year		Percent of Functional Allocation (Current Year)							Coming Year		Percent of Functional Allocation (Coming Year)						
		(1)	(2)	(3)	(4)	(5)	(6)	(7)	(8)		(1)	(2)	(3)	(4)	(5)	(6)	(7)	(8)
Sunday Services																		
8:00	4,207	15	20	10	5	—	—	5	5	4,427	15	20	10	5	—	5	5	5
9:15	6,985	30	20	35	40	—	—	40	40	7,491	30	20	35	40	—	40	40	40
11:30	6,985	30	20	35	40	—	—	40	40	7,491	30	20	35	40	—	40	40	40
Vespers	4,285	15	20	10	10	—	—	10	10	4,545	15	20	10	10	—	10	10	10
Midweek	3,527	10	20	10	5	—	—	5	5	3,709	10	20	10	5	—	5	5	5
Total	25,989									27,663								

Functions

Functions	Current Year		Percent of Total Functional Expense (Current Year)							Coming Year		Percent of Total Functional Expense (Coming Year)						
		(1)	(2)	(3)	(4)	(5)	(6)	(7)	(8)		(1)	(2)	(3)	(4)	(5)	(6)	(7)	(8)
1. Personnel	13,610	52								14,368	52							
2. Facilities	10,060		39							10,600		38						
3. Equipment	754			3						350			1					
4. Supplies/Postage	1,388				5					1,980				7				
5. Gifts & Grants	—					—				—					—			
6. Training	—						—			175						1		
7. Books & Periodicals	139							1		150							1	
8. Miscellaneous	38								—	40								—
Total	25,989									27,663								
% of Total Budget	16.41									16.08								

Exhibit 4-5—Functions Section of a Programs/Functions Budget

Personnel Expense	Current Year		Coming Year	
Pastor	$ 32,000		$ 35,000	
Associate Pastor	14,000		15,600	
Secretary	8,700		9,500	
Custodian	7,000		7,000	
Christian Education Director	4,800		5,500	
Organist	2,700		3,000	
Service Choir Director	2,000		2,000	
Junior Choir Director	10,000		1,000	
Total Personnel Expense		$72,200		$78,600
% of Total Budget		45.61		45.70
Facilities Expense				
Debt Service	30,500		30,000	
Utilities	10,500		12,000	
Maintenance	6,000		7,500	
Insurance	3,300		3,500	
Total Facilities Expense		$50,300		$53,000
% of Total Budget		31.78		30.81
Equipment Expense				
Purchases	1,100		2,200	
Debt Service	1,020		1,000	
Operating Expenses	2,700		3,500	
Insurance	250		300	
Total Equipment Expense		$5,070		$7,000
% of Total Budget		3.20		4.07
Supplies and Postage				
Supplies	8,600		9,000	
Postage	840		900	
Total Supplies & Postage		$9,440		$9,900
% of Total Budget		5.96		5.76
Gifts and Grants				
Cooperative Program	9,100		9,200	
World Mission	450		500	
Local Mission	6,000		7,100	
Honoraria	200		500	
Total Gifts & Grants		$15,750		$17,300
% of Total Budget		9.95		10.06

Training	Current Year		Coming Year	
Total Training		$700		$1,200
% of Total Budget		0.44		0.70
Books & Periodicals				
Books	375		400	
Periodicals	180		200	
Total Books & Periodicals		$555		$600
% of Total Budget		0.35		0.35
Miscellaneous				
Assessment	3,300		3,600	
Conference Expense	600		400	
Audit	375		400	
Total Miscellaneous		$4,275		$4,400
% of Total Budget		2.70		2.56
Total Budget		$158,290		$172,000

7. *Board Review of Preliminary Budget.* The primary purpose of this step is to present the completed proposed budget (with any revisions motivated by the congregational review) to the governing board.

8. *Implement the Canvass Plan.* (This assumes that the church employs the annual canvass approach to fund raising. If not, these subsections on canvassing can be skipped.) The canvass director will have been planning the canvass and organizing the canvass team during the preliminary stages of the budget preparation procedure. At this point all the canvass director needs to do is to put his or her plan into operation.

9. *Begin Canvass.* If the canvass has been well planned and the canvass team well organized and prepared, this step should be taken automatically. It is important, however, that the canvass be started early enough so that final results are in hand at least one month and

Exhibit 4-6   Coming Year Income Expectations

Expected Operating Income
[1]Expected coming year income
  from pledges $123,500

[2]Expected income from delinquent
  pledges   2,500
[2]Expected loose plate collections   7,000
[3]Expected income from grants   3,500
[4]Expected interest income   3,000

Expected Operating Income $139,500

Expected Building Fund Income
[5]Expected coming year income from
  building fund pledges   30,000
[2]Expected income from delinquent
  building fund pledges   500

Expected Building Fund Income   30,500
Total anticipated income in the coming year   170,000
Proposed budget in the coming year   172,000

Deficit   ($2,000)

Documentation
1. Actual pledges totaled $130,000. The pledges were multiplied
    by a factor of 0.95 to reflect the fact that not all pledge
    commitments will be kept. The collection factor is based on the
    last five years' experience.
2. This estimate was obtained by calculating the average amount
    received for each of the first nine months of the year and
    multiplying that by twelve to annualize it and then multiplying it
    by another factor to account for an upward trend experienced
    over the last five years.
3. This figure is based on a contractual agreement.
4. This figure is based on the assumption that no changes are made
    in the church's investment portfolio and that interest rates will
    remain unchanged.
5. Actual pledges of $30,612.25 were multiplied by a factor of 0.98
    to reflect the fact that not all building fund pledges have been
    met in the past.

preferably forty-five days prior to the start of a new fiscal year.

10. *Conclude Canvass.* It is useful to show a specific termination date to motivate canvass team members to get started and to ensure that the canvass does not drag on and on.

11. *Construct a Pro Forma Income Statement.* A *pro forma* income statement is a projection of revenues anticipated in the coming year. Certain basic principles govern the construction of a *pro forma.* First, it should be simple in format and easy to understand. (Remember that not everyone on the governing board is a financial expert.) Second, a *pro forma* should identify *all* sources of expected revenue. Third, the *pro forma* should include documentation of all the numbers in the statement as well as the assumptions upon which the numbers are based. Fourth, it should include a comparison of anticipated revenues with the budget.

An example of a *pro forma* income statement is shown in Exhibit 4-6. Notice that all sources of income have been identified and that straightforward documentation of assumptions is included. More details than are shown in the sample exhibit probably should not be included. Instead, additional information ought to be supplied orally in response to questions raised at the board review of the *pro forma.*

Several items in Exhibit 4-6 merit discussion. The weighting factors used to discount general fund and building fund pledges would normally be based on historical collection percentages, but a downward adjustment in these figures would be appropriate if the local economy were expected to decline during the coming fiscal year. Expected income from delinquent pledges and loose plate should reflect trends experienced in the past. Normally growth would be anticipated; but given adverse circumstances, such as a decrease in membership or a decline in the local economy, shrinkage might be expected. Upward adjustment would be in order if unforeseen happy events occurred.

Observe that the sample *pro forma* income statement shows a deficit. In this event it is helpful for the budget director to prepare two lists:

1. Potential new sources of funds which can be tapped to eliminate the deficit.
2. Line items which are the best candidates for cuts in terms of their absolute size and their importance to the church's program.

5. *Employing a marketing mix.* Earlier the expression "marketing mix" was used. Let us define the mix here as "the set of factors influencing consumer demand for a company's product over which it has some degree of control." Usually, the mix would include advertising, personal selling, sales promotion (such as contests, coupons, free samples, fancy displays), product quality and features, pricing, and distribution. (Whether to market a product direct to retailers or to wholesalers and then to retailers is a question of distribution.) For the company, marketing mix decisions are tactical. Examples of tactical marketing decisions are how much money to spend on advertising, what media to use, and the timing of advertising placement (June vs. December, for example). Another example of a marketing mix decision in the area of sales promotion is whether to introduce a new product by using a free sample or a coupon.

The marketing-oriented church also employs a coordinated set of marketing tactics which is in harmony with its basic strategy. Although the church's marketing mix differs in particulars from the marketing mix of a company, the basic components are similar. Where the company might use advertising and personal selling to communicate with its customers, the marketing-oriented church utilizes mass communications media such as bulletins, newsletters, mailouts, and advertising. It also employs interpersonal communications methods which are similar to personal selling (consider the annual canvass as one example).

Another component of the church's marketing mix is sales promotion (which is employed by business firms to gain product trial, to forestall competition, to attract attention, and to build organizational morale). Consider some examples of church "promotions," such as fairs and bazaars, revivals, contests, and attendance prizes. These events and awards are clearly promotional and are conducted for many of the same reasons promotions are conducted by business firms. They are normally well publicized; they often result in increased church membership, and they almost always build morale.

"Product policy" is also an element of the church's marketing mix, although one which is given too little emphasis. The church's "products" are its major programs—for example, youth fellowship groups or Christian education—and the specific activities which are represented in major programs. The marketing-oriented church should take a systematic approach both to the discovery and

If line item requests have been separated into essential and discretionary components, the budget director should have little difficulty identifying line items which can be cut with a minimum of pain and suffering.

12. *Board Review of Pro Forma Income Statement.* At this meeting the *pro forma* income statement is presented to the church's governing board. In the event that the *pro forma* shows a budget deficit, it is up to the board either to accept the budget, conditional on the expectation that additional funds can be raised to eliminate the deficit, or to make selective cuts in the budget. If the *pro forma* shows a budget surplus, the board should determine how the surplus is to be applied. In any event, the board should adopt a budget for the coming year.

13. *Construction of the Actual Budget.* Once the coming year's budget has been accepted by the board, actual commitment of the budget to paper is a clerical and secretarial task following the formats previously adopted.

Financial Control

In this section monthly and quarterly financial reporting are discussed. Both forms of reporting are necessary for controlling financial activities within the church, but each form serves a different purpose.

Monthly Financial Reporting

Monthly financial reports should provide information on income and expenditures. They should also indicate financial performance relative to plan and performance relative to available historical data.

Exhibit 4-7 is a sample monthly income summary. It shows major income categories and breakdowns associated with those categories. Notice that five columns of figures are included:

1. The first two columns show actual income for the month and a cumulative total.
2. The next columns show three sets of cumulative percentages:
    a) actual relative to budget,
    b) the percentage anticipated when the annual financial plan was constructed (this percentage can be determined rather easily from the cash flow projections shown in the budget request forms),

Exhibit 4-7—Monthly Income Summary

Monthly Income Summary
Month: April

Income Category	Actual Income		Cumulative Percentages		
	This Month	Cumulative	Actual	Plan	Historical
General Fund					
Current year pledges	$10,125	$41,875	32.21%	35%	31.92%
Prior year pledges	23	1,830	73.20	97	90.38
Loose plate	684	2,823	40.33	42	42.34
Grants income	0	825	23.57	24	(a)
Interest income	50	800	26.67	27	25.00
Building Fund					
Current year pledges	2,225	8,750	29.17	35	32.84
Prior year pledges	0	0	0	95	85.66

Notes

(a) The church has not previously received any grants.

     c) the historical percentages for each income category when historical data are available.

When needed for purposes of clarification, notes are also included in the summary.

Although an actual monthly financial summary would include many numbers, we think the detail is useful. Showing each separate source of revenue ("Income Category") permits remedial action to be taken quickly if problems arise. If income data are considered in the aggregate, potential problem areas often cannot be identified in time to take remedial action. Figures showing actual income for the month reflect the relative significance of each income source. Actual cumulative income provides a useful basis for interpretation of the percentages shown in columns 3, 4, and 5.

Consider the percentages in Exhibit 4-7. Comparisons of "actual" and "plan" percentages serve two useful purposes. First, if the plan figure is realistic, a substantial difference between actual and plan signals a potential problem. Second, if the plan figure is unrealistic (lack of realism might be perceived in a sizable difference between plan and historical), a modification in the procedure for obtaining the plan percentage would be in order. Historical percentages are frequently quite useful for measuring performance and should be the basis for plan figures in many instances. For example, monthly collections often are not uniform throughout the year (because of tax payments or vacation expenditures by members of the congregation, for example), but the basic pattern is likely to be stable from one year to the next. In cases of this sort, comparing the actual income percentage with a plan figure based on an improper assumption that revenue is the same from month to month can easily lead to unnecessary concern.

Observe that most of the numbers in Exhibit 4-7 are based on the concept of cumulative income, that is, income for January, then income for January and February, then income for January, February, and March, etc. The use of cumulatives helps the reader avoid paying undue attention to a single anomalous month which will tend to be averaged out over time. Really serious problems are usually experienced over several months. If desired, however, percentages for a single month may be easily determined by subtracting last month's cumulative from this month's cumulative. For example, in the figure the April cumulative percentage of actual

income is 32.31. If the March cumulative percentage had been
23.60, the single month percentage for April would be 32.21 −
23.60 = 8.61 percent. An additional advantage of cumulatives is
that they quite naturally lead the reader of financial statements to
make projections to the end of the year—a useful and managerially
responsible activity.

Exhibits 4-8 and 4-9 are two segments from a "reporting budget."
The reporting budget corresponds closely to the programs/func-
tions planning budget format seen earlier in Exhibits 4-4 and 4-5 in
terms of category class and layout. That is, the reporting budget
includes breakdowns by program with further breakdowns by
activity and broad function under program. The reporting budget is
also broken down by function into individual expenditure
categories.

The reporting budget, like the programs/functions planning
budget, is designed to be a tool for financial *and* operating
management. In terms of the data shown the reporting budget also
corresponds to the monthly income summary in Exhibit 4-8.
Because of the similarities in data format between Exhibit 4-7 and
Exhibits 4-8 and 4-9, little added discussion is required. We only
draw the reader's attention to the asterisks in the last column in
Exhibits 4-8 and 4-9. They call attention to items of possible
concern. Use of this "exception reporting" technique permits the
governing board member to have access to all the relevant
information yet still economize on his or her time. There are no
universally accepted rules for deciding which items should or should
not be starred, but the actual amount of the item in question, the
relative size of the deviation from plan or historical experience, and
the number of periods during which a large deviation has been
observed would all be important criteria for making the choice.

The Quarterly Pro Forma

Quarterly *pro formas* should be prepared at the end of the first,
second, and third quarters. Their basic purpose is to show members
of the governing board, clergy, and business manager what the
end-of-year financial condition of the church is likely to be if trends
observable at the end of each quarter are maintained throughout
the year. A well-constructed quarterly *pro forma* is most useful in
the event of serious revenue shortfalls or expense overruns because
a problem is highlighted early enough for corrective action to be

Exhibit 4-8   Reporting Budget Segment for Missions

Program: Missions
Month: April

Category / Activities	Actual Expenditures		Cumulative Percentages			Exceptions
	This Month	Cumu- lative	Actual	Plan	Historical	
Cooperative Program	$820	$3,280	33%	33%	33%	
World Mission	—	752	50	50	67	* *
Local Mission						
Contact	747	2,429	38	33	37	
People in Need	898	2,295	51	20	15	
Hospital House	546	2,074	38	40	43	
Benevolences	130	332	22	20	33	
Total	3,141	11,162				

Function						*	*
Personnel	$800	$2,970	40%	33%	35%		
Facilities	221	875	33	33	33		
Equipment	58	231	33	33	40		
Supplies & Postage	71	248	25	33	30		
Gifts & Grants	1,661	6,425	38	33	30		
Training	300	300	100	100	10		
Books & Periodicals	10	40	33	33	36		
Miscellaneous	20	73	33	33	33		
Total	3,141	11,162					

Exhibit 4-9   Reporting Budget Segment for Equipment

Function: Equipment
Month: April

Category	Actual Expenditures		Cumulative Percentages			Exceptions
	This Month	Cumu-lative	Actual	Plan	Historical	*
Purchases	$215	$1,320	60%	—%	30%	
Debt Service	83	333	33	33	36	
Operating Expense	318	1,470	42	38	40	
Insurance	160	210	80	80	50	
Total	776	3,333	48	27	38	

taken with a minimum of dislocation. The quarterly *pro forma* is particularly useful during periods of economic recession.

On a more positive note, the quarterly *pro forma* can also signal a coming budget surplus. With advance notice that additional funds are likely to be forthcoming, well-considered decisions can be made in the area of program expansion, an approach most would find preferable to an often lightly considered end-of-year decision to "dump" money on some outside program in order to avoid the embarrassment of a large budget surplus.

On the income portion the quarterly *pro forma's* format should follow closely the format of the "Coming Year Income Expectations" *pro forma* shown in Exhibit 4-6. The major difference between the income component of the quarterly *pro forma* in Exhibit 4-10 and the one in Exhibit 4-6 is in the numbers shown, the quarterly *pro forma* being constructed using the latest information on actual income. As a consequence, it should be a better predictor of end-of-year results.

The expense side of the quarterly *pro forma* is also represented in Exhibit 4-10. The exhibit shows an expected deficit of $1,820. When combined with expected revenues of $172,005, the *pro forma* predicts an end-of-year deficit of $1,815. The third section of the exhibit shows the significant expected overspending and underspending which, when combined, produced the anticipated deficit. Two more points pertaining to the construction of quarterly *pro formas* are in order:

1. Only those items which are significantly out of control should be included, that is, items which by their magnitude or by the size of their deviation from plan can have a large effect on budget as a whole.
2. Exhibit 4-10 includes only five broadly defined items. In actual practice items would be more numerous and more clearly identified.

On the technical side, there are several methods for making estimates of over- and underspending. One approach would be to project an observed partial-year difference between actual and *planned* cumulative expenditure to the end of the year. For example, if at the end of the second quarter the actual cumulative percentage expenditure on an item was 35 percent and the planned cumulative expenditure was 40 percent, the expected end-of-year

Exhibit 4-10—Second Quarterly Pro Forma Revenue

Expected Operating Income

[1]Expected coming year income from pledges	$126,900	
[2]Expected income from delinquent pledges	1,885	
[2]Expected loose plate collections	6,720	
[3]Expected income from grants	3,500	
[4]Expected interest income	3,000	
Expected Operating Income		$142,005

Expected Building Fund Income

[5]Expected coming year income from building fund pledges	$ 30,000	
[2]Expected income from delinquent building fund pledges	0	
Expected Building Fund Income		30,000
Total anticipated income in the coming year		$172,005

EXPENSES

Current year's budget	$172,000	
Expected budget deficit	(1,820)	$173,820
Expected deficit		($ 1,815)

EXPECTED OVER- AND UNDERSPENDING

Expected Overspending

Item	% Overspent	Amount Overspent
Utilities	10.8%	$ 1,300
Purchases	31.8	700
Postage	16.7	150
Conference expense	31.3	125
Total Overspending		($ 2,275)

Expected Underspending

Insurance (Equipment)	18.33%	$ 55
Honoraria	80.00	400
Total Underspending		$ 455
Balance		($ 1,820)

Exhibit 4-10 (continued)

Documentation
1. Three members of the congregation agreed to increase their pledges enough to eliminate the budget deficit anticipated prior to this fiscal year so that actual pledges are $135,000. This figure has been multiplied by a factor of 0.94, our best judgment at this time of the proportion of pledge commitments that will be kept.
2. This estimate was obtained by dividing actual income received by the "plan" percentage expressed as a proportion.
3. This figure is based on a contractual arrangement.
4. This figure is based on the assumption that no changes are made in the church's investment portfolio for the remaining six months of the year and that interest rates remain unchanged.
5. Actual collections relative to pledges support our original assumption that 2 percent of the pledges will be delinquent ($30,612.25 \times 0.98 = $30,000$).

cumulative percentage of expenditure would be 35/40 × 100 = 87.5 percent, and the expected underspending percentage would be 12.5 percent. To determine the *amount underspent,* the figure of 12.5 would be applied to the original budgeted amount. A related method would employ a projection of the relative difference between actual and historical cumulative percentages to the end of the year.

Financial Planning and Control with Minicomputers

All the financial planning and control documents shown in the exhibits in this chapter can be produced on the office typewriter. However, they are time consuming for the church secretary to prepare. When these documents are programmed on a minicomputer or word processor, they can be produced easily and inexpensively. Also changes can be made with a minimum of effort.

At this point the reader is probably thinking, *I knew there was a trick here—you need a computer to produce all these reports, and our church can't possibly afford one.* The financial documents shown in this chapter need not be produced on a computer or word processor. However, amazing breakthroughs in the electronics field have caused a drastic reduction in computer prices in recent years. Even now the large church (with, for example, a budget in excess of $300,000) may find that a small minicomputer can pay for itself. Before many more years pass, the medium-sized church will discover that the minicomputer is as essential to the church office as the ubiquitous electric typewriter and copying machine are now.

There are some steps the forward-looking pastor can take to move the church into the world of the computer. First, and most important, the pastor should identify those individuals in the congregation who have computer-related jobs (there are probably few churches in America that do not have at least one programmer or systems analyst in the congregation). Second, ask members of the congregation whose work brings them in day-to-day contact with the computer to serve on an advisory committee whose job it would be to analyze all church activities to determine which ones can be usefully computerized. Finally, ask members of the committee if they will investigate the feasibility of the church's acquiring a computer (or, and perhaps better, renting slack time on a business or university computer that is underutilized at certain times of the day or week).

Chapter 5

Applying Marketing Principles
to Outreach Programs

For those of us working outside the business world, the term "marketing" usually means advertising and personal selling. These two activities are often equated with the marketing function as a whole because they touch our daily lives so frequently. Marketing is much more than advertising and personal selling, however. As Philip Kotler points out, marketing's job is to *facilitate exchanges* between people, between organizations, or between people and organizations—marketing does not so much involve a specific set of skills, methods, policies, and institutional arrangements as it does a way of doing things.[1]

At first glance much of the terminology permeating traditional marketing literature would seem inappropriate or unrelated to the functions of a church and its outreach programs. Taking the opposite point of view, it is our belief that the terminology and, more importantly, underlying principles and techniques are not only appropriate to the outreach functions of the church but they are also essential. Indeed, we will go so far as to state that, relative to churches in general, marketing-oriented churches are more sensitive than other churches to the needs of the members of the congregation as well as to the needs of other groups with which churches interact.

We begin by attempting to capture the meaning of business marketing in seven statements which are then translated into the

---

[1]Philip Kotler, *Marketing Management*, 4th ed. (Englewood Cliffs, N.J.: Prentice-Hall, Inc., 1980), p. 19.

church's situation. In the next section a number of suggestions are made about how marketing principles and techniques can be applied to the church. A brief list of practical marketing references is included in the Bibliography for those interested in learning more about the subject and how to put it to work in the service of the Almighty. This chapter may lead church leaders into what may seem to be unfamiliar territory. Persevere—the utility of the concepts unfolds as you read on.

The Meaning of Marketing

The marketing-oriented business firm can be defined in terms of seven distinguishing characteristics:

1. It is sensitive to the needs of its consumers.
2. It identifies homogeneous groups of consumers and designs marketing programs to serve them.
3. It specifies quantifiable objectives and clearly articulated strategies.
4. It facilitates the flow of information to and from consumers.
5. It adopts a marketing mix (a term to be defined later) best suited to its customers, its strengths, and its resources.
6. It follows a marketing plan.
7. It controls and evaluates marketing programs.

Now let's translate these statements into seven related statements which characterize the "marketing-oriented" church (A reader uncomfortable with the term "marketing-oriented" might substitute "outreach-oriented." We are comfortable with either term but use marketing-oriented because this is, after all, a chapter on church marketing and because the connection between the marketing activities of companies and churches should be made as obvious as possible.):

1. It develops and maintains sensitivity to parishioners.
2. It identifies and serves homogeneous groups inside and outside the church.
3. It specifies numerical objectives and clearly stated strategies for church programs and activities.
4. It emphasizes information flows to and from its publics.
5. It employs marketing tactics to enhance program success.

6. It prepares and follows a marketing plan.
7. It controls and evaluates its marketing program.

In the following paragraphs each characteristic is briefly explained.

1. *Developing and maintaining parishioner sensitivity.* In contrast to the old "sell 'em what you got" philosophy, today's sophisticated business marketers know that their chances of success are far greater if they find out exactly what consumers want and then produce products and services to fulfill those wants. Similarly, in the religious sphere, the marketing-oriented church does not take its congregation for granted. It *systematically* determines who its parishioners are and the nature of their spiritual, material, and social needs. At some initial point in time it asks questions of members of the congregation, and it gets answers. Then periodically the questions are asked again. What kinds of questions might be asked? Here are some examples:

- How old are members of the congregation?
- Where do they live?
- Where do they work?
- How many children do they have, and what are their ages?
- Where do the children go to school?
- Where do they go to college?
- Do they like variety and change in services, or do they prefer a more traditional approach?
- What benefits do parishioners expect from their church?
- What do parishioners think is expected of them in return?
- Why do parishioners go to this church?
- What are the problems of churchgoing in general?
- What are the problems of going to this church in particular?

With the answers to these questions before them, church leaders can design and implement the kinds of programs which successfully fill the needs of the many groups the church serves.

2. *Finding and serving homogeneous groups.* It is not enough today for the business firm to know what products and services consumers want *generally*, because there can be important differences in specific wants from one group of consumers to another even though in general desires are much the same. Similarly, the marketing-oriented church should identify relatively

homogeneous groups within the congregation, determine their special needs, and then meet those needs within the church's overall strategy. In order to apply a policy of identifying and serving homogeneous groups, the church leader must realize that he or she has a farm rather than a flock. Some of the people in the congregation are sheep, granted, but others are cattle and horses. (And, perhaps, some are even goats!) Treating all animals on a farm as if they were sheep would surely produce bad results. Can't a similar statement be made about a church?

3. *Specifying numerical objectives and clearly stated strategies.* (The reader will note many similarities between concepts in this chapter and those in chapters dealing with planning. Marketing and financial and personnel management all utilize the same concepts, and much information is common to all.) One gains the impression that church leaders rarely attempt to specify marketing objectives at all, let alone objectives stated in quantifiable terms. Similarly, they don't appear to realize that they are following a marketing strategy, even if it's just the one implicit in the church's operating style. When objectives are not clearly specified and church leaders do not adopt explicit, written marketing strategies, implicit strategies which often fit the church, its congregation, and its time and locality rather well are traded in for other, more faddish methods of operation. The frequent result of poor strategy combined with the absence of clearly specified objectives is a decline in membership and financial support. To be truly marketing oriented, church leaders should define strategies unambiguously, and the results anticipated from strategy components should be stated as expected numerical and percentage changes.

4. *Emphasizing information flows.* The marketing-oriented church reaches out to listen and to inform. It manages the flow of information to and from its publics in the sense that a specified individual is responsible for the church's overall communication program. In practical terms, emphasizing information flows means that a systematic but inexpensive procedure is constructed to learn about members of the congregation, about the aspects of the church they particularly like, and about the aspects with which they are dissatisfied. Finally, emphasizing information flows implies that all forms of mass communication, such as bulletins, newsletters, and advertising should be coordinated in terms of appearance, purpose, and quality level.

development of new product ideas and to the abandonment of products (programs) which have outlived their usefulness. (See chapter 8 of Kotler's book, *Marketing for Nonprofit Organizations,* for some useful suggestions on how to establish a product policy.)[2]

The "price" element of the church's marketing mix differs markedly from the corresponding element in the marketing mix of a firm because churches don't normally charge a dollar price for their programs. However, there is an implicit price involved with religious activity which churches frequently ignore: the time required of individuals who provide or consume the services produced in church programs.

If a program requires hours and hours of meetings or is held at an inconvenient time or place, its "time price" is high. When activities have high time prices, reduced participation can be expected. Conversely, when time prices are low, participation levels should be high. The key point here is that, where possible, church leaders should attempt to lower time prices of church programs. If substantial time input reductions are achieved with no reduction in services received from programs and if the reductions are well publicized, increased participation should result. Similarly, when a church contemplates mounting a new program, serious consideration should be given to its expected time price and how the price can be minimized.

Distribution strategy is an important element of the church's marketing mix, and the criterion for selecting a distribution channel option for a given program is similar to that of the business firm: provide a program to the greatest number of parishioners at the lowest cost to them and to the organization providing the program. The marketing-oriented church may wish to adopt several channel strategies to meet the criterion of maximum consumer satisfaction at minimum cost. For example, although programs of worship would normally be distributed directly to parishioners, community action program support in terms of money, goods, and contributed time might be distributed most effectively through a service organization located where the needs are (a Salvation Army mission, for example).

[2]Philip Kotler, *Marketing for Nonprofit Organizations* (Englewood Cliffs, N.J.: Prentice-Hall, Inc., 1975), chapter 8.

6. *Preparing and implementing a marketing plan.* The church's marketing plan should incorporate an overview of the situation, a statement of objectives, a description of the strategy or strategies to be followed, and details about the tactics necessary to achieve goals. These details include specific activities to be accomplished, dates, individuals responsible, and resource needs. The church marketing plan should also indicate benchmarks to be accomplished and the dates when measurements should be taken. Essentially a church marketing plan is a component of the strategic plan for the church. (Planning concepts are discussed in chapters 2 and 3.)

7. *Controlling and evaluating the marketing program.* Control involves establishing appropriate benchmarks for marketing programs and then ensuring that they're met. Benchmarks are established in the marketing plan. They may be stated in terms of the results anticipated from an activity by a specific date. For other activities where specification of results is unnecessary or inappropriate, benchmarks are best stated in terms of task accomplishment. For control to be effective, intermediate goals must be achievable, performance must be measured; and when benchmarks are not reached, questions must be raised. (These concepts of control and evaluation are discussed in more depth in chapter 3.)

Putting Ideas to Work

In this section we offer several specific, practical proposals to enable a church to become more marketing oriented. Because of space limitations, a broad-brush approach is taken. Only the outlines of procedures are given, leaving the details to be filled in from two general sources: (1) books and periodicals listed in the Bibliography, and (2) marketing professionals in the church's own congregation. Issues considered in this section are: image, organization, target groups definition, and differentiated marketing. Several of these concepts have been borrowed from the now-classic article on marketing in nonprofit organizations by Kotler and Levy.[3]

The Problem and Opportunity of "Image"

"Image" is best defined as the church's personality. Image is the

---

[3]Philip Kotler and Sidney J. Levy, "Broadening the Concept of Marketing," *Journal of Marketing*, vol. 33, no. 1 (January, 1969), pp. 10-15.

picture that comes to mind when the church's name is mentioned. It
is generally considered to be based on a number of characteristics of
the church, its program, and its congregation.

How often have you heard one church described as "cold and
aloof" and another as a "warm and friendly place"? The first
church's image is obviously negative, and its leaders would surely
try to change the image *if they knew the church was perceived as a
cold and an aloof place.* The church in the second example has a
positive image. *If leaders of that church were aware of its image,*
they'd surely work to maintain and enhance it.

A negative image makes it difficult for a church to replenish its
membership and achieve program objectives. On the other hand, a
positive image supports steady congregational growth, enhances
the church's ability to reach program goals, and brings people to
services on Sunday. A church's image may not be truly
representative of reality, but more often than not it is an accurate, if
somewhat incomplete, snapshot of a more complete and detailed
structure. If a church has a negative image, in most cases there are
important characteristics of its facilities, its programs, its congregation, or its surroundings that are viewed unfavorably by a
significant number of people.

Image is difficult to change; change is a slow process, and
permanent change can be accomplished only by changing
underlying factors. Temporary changes in image may be accomplished by changing communications tactics, however. To the
extent that such modifications are only cosmetic and don't reflect
substantive changes in underlying factors, they may produce
disastrous results with the church being perceived even more
negatively after the image change is attempted.

Before image can be modified, it should be accurately measured.
Several types of attitude scales have been developed for this
purpose. A questionnaire with statements like the examples is
helpful:

Centerville Church is a progressive church

Strongly   1   2   3   4   5   6   Strongly
Agree   Disagree

The congregation of Centerville Church is young

Strongly   1   2   3   4   5   6   Strongly
Agree   Disagree

Other approaches are equally effective. The interested reader is advised to consult books by Kotler[4] and Churchill[5] for guidance in the construction of attitude scales. The main point to be made here is that church leaders should have a valid assessment at hand before any attempt is made to change a negative image or to use a positive image as a framework for marketing strategy development.

Constructing a Marketing Organization

Ideally the marketing-oriented church should have a marketing organization corresponding to the marketing organization of a business firm. It should have a chief marketing officer and individuals responsible for mass communication (both internal and external media), for interpersonal communication (personal contact), for information acquisition (surveys and monitoring of external developments), and for programs (development of new programs and evaluation of old ones). Such an organizational structure is represented in the chart shown in Exhibit 5-1.

Exhibit 5-1

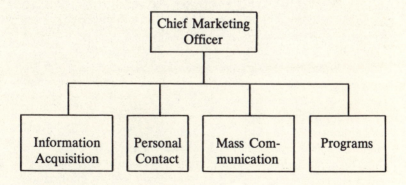

Normally the pastor is the church's chief marketing officer (in very large churches an associate pastor or business manager might

[4]Kotler, *op. cit.,* chapter 7.
[5]Gilbert A. Churchill, Jr., *Marketing Research: Methodological Foundations* (Hinsdale, Ill.: Dryden Press, imprint of Holt, Rinehart & Winston, 1976), chapter 7.

perform this function). Whichever church leader serves as chief marketing officer, building a marketing organization should not be difficult for it will be discovered that many existing committees already perform the functions depicted in Exhibit 5-1.

Implementation of the functional organizational structure may just involve changing some committee names and adding new responsibilities or subtracting old ones. Alternatively, and perhaps more wisely, committee names and structure may be retained, but tasks and responsibilities may be reassigned from one committee to another (or added in cases where they were previously nonexistent). If the church's committee structure doesn't correspond to the exhibit and a decision is made to alter the structure, the leaders of the church have a more difficult task. To get the job done in this case, employ the three *p's*: planning, patience, and perseverance! Useful suggestions for constructing a marketing organization in a nonprofit organization may be found in a recent article by Kotler.[6]

The organizational structure shown in Exhibit 5-1 is uncluttered and has direct lines of authority. This type of simple structure may be used by the very large church where committees (and perhaps subcommittees) report to each of the functional directors shown in the exhibit. It may also be used by the very small church where a single lay leader performs more than one of the functions shown. Regardless of the size of the organization, it is essential that functions are clearly defined and effectively performed.

In the following paragraphs the purpose of each function in the marketing organization exhibit is discussed. In addition, recommendations are made for accomplishing the objectives associated with each of the functions.

Information acquisition. The committee responsible for information acquisition is the church's eyes and ears. It is responsible for collecting, processing, and interpreting data to establish policies and design programs. One of the responsibilities of the information acquisition committee is to maintain a profile on each individual and household in the congregation. Facts useful for constructing a profile are age, occupation, number of children, educational accomplishment, employer, previous place of residence, and length of time in the congregation. Addresses are also useful because they show the "neighborhood" of the church (the area from which it

[6]Philip Kotler, "Strategies for Introducing Marketing into Nonprofit Organizations," *Journal of Marketing,* vol. 43, no. 1 (January, 1979), pp. 37-44.

draws parishioners) and the average distances members of the congregation travel to and from church. It is important to know about the church's neighborhood to anticipate the effects of change resulting from local area population shifts. Distance traveled may have an important impact on the program attendance, especially as energy costs increase relative to prices of other commodities.

It is important to know the characteristics of the congregation, but it is equally as important to determine how church members perceive the church and its programs. General attitudes are normally best measured in small group sessions held in the homes of church members. These sessions should not be completely open-ended, and some direction is productive. A guide sheet should be used for that purpose by the leader of small group sessions. Normally eight to twelve participants will produce good interaction.

Answers to specific questions can be obtained using the more formal questionnaire approach. In terms of representativeness of the sample of respondents, speed of completion, and expense, the best results are obtained from telephone surveys. If mail is used, however, be sure to follow up. Two cautions about collecting information are in order. First, unless a crucial issue has arisen, don't overdo direct information gathering; conducting a comprehensive survey once every three years is probably sufficient. Second, seek the help of an experienced research professional before group interviews or surveys are conducted; results will be better. Such persons are often found in the congregations of large churches. Other sources of help with surveys are denominational offices and departments of business, economics, psychology, or sociology at nearby colleges or universities. Students in these departments are often looking for opportunities to do survey research in the community, and they can produce good results at a low cost. Also faculty members at local colleges and universities frequently consult in these areas.

Other useful information acquisition activities are collecting data on trends and issues in religion at the local, denominational, and ecumenical levels. At the local level, activities of other churches can be monitored through their bulletins and newsletters. These media provide good program ideas and may help the church avoid scheduling conflicts with major events of other churches. Obviously bulletins and newsletters from other churches may also serve as models for a church's own communications media.

Church leaders can maintain an awareness of events taking place at the denominational level by examining information from the denomination's offices. Awareness of events in the wider sphere of religion in national life can be maintained by monitoring the more general religious literature. Local denominational and national sources of information should be examined *regularly and systematically*. To accomplish this objective, divide up the monitoring task so that each individual responsible for information acquisition has only a small and easily managed part of the total job. Recognize time pressures. Give each member of the committee only as much work to do as can be done comfortably, and avoid duplication in assignments. Each member of the committee should screen only a part of all the information flowing to the church. Important items should be abstracted and made available to church leaders and to the committee as a whole.

Personal contact. The personal contact committee is the church's sales organization. It is responsible for recruiting, training, and motivating the volunteer workers needed to staff church programs. This committee should also be responsible for actively managing "people-to-people" activities, such as the annual canvass and evangelism programs.

One benefit of having personal contact confined to a single committee is that, through their experiences, members become specialists. Another benefit is that members of the committee can more easily keep tabs on the activities of all volunteer workers so that the church's work can be more equitably shared.

Because the sales management function is the activity in business most resembling the management of personal contact activities in voluntary organizations, the literature on selling and sales management is a useful source of ideas, principles, and techniques. Books about motivating volunteers are also helpful (also see chapter 8). If there is a sales manager in the congregation, solicit his or her help in establishing a personal contact committee.

Mass communication. The committee performing this function might also be called the publications or public relations committee. Its primary purpose is coordinating all the church's mass communications media to ensure timeliness, quality of production, and consistency of format. Committee members would be responsible for the design and format of bulletins, newsletters, mass mailings, and advertising.

To staff this committee, the same basic principles recommended for staffing other committees should be followed. In this particular case, however, individuals from the congregation should be recruited who have experience in advertising or public relations. Alternatively, those who have TV, radio, or newspaper experience have good potential. Clearly the best results can be obtained by appointing experienced committee leaders, but, experienced or not, members of this committee would benefit from reading literature about advertising and public relations practice. Also advertising and public relations seminars are useful, particularly those having a practical orientation (some of which may be specifically oriented to the needs of nonprofit organizations).

Programs. This committee's primary responsibility is new program development and the evaluation of ongoing programs. In the development area, studying the feasibility of mounting programs similar to those in other churches (discovered by the information acquisition committee) would be a task of this committee. The committee would also evaluate interchurch and interdenominational programs to determine whether participation in such programs would be appropriate.

This committee would also assist in program implementation by providing funding, facilities, personnel, and organizational advice. When someone in the church has that great new program idea, the programs committee provides the assistance necessary to get it up and running quickly.

Although the primary purposes of the programs committee would be screening, developing, and providing support for new programs, another major purpose would be the annual evaluation of existing church programs. Evaluation should be conducted in the late spring when the church year is winding down and time demands of programs are lower. Each church program should be scrutinized with attention to program mission, success in accomplishing the mission, resource requirements, and overlap with other programs in the church or community. After assessing the performance of each program and activity, the programs committee should make one of three recommendations to the governing board: (1) continue with no change in operations, (2) continue with specific changes (the need for which would be fully documented), or (3) discontinue (and here again the recommendation would be fully documented). Chapter 3 provides more specifics on this evaluation process.

Defining Target Groups

Target groups are identifiable groups of individuals with common needs or interests and, more often than not, homogeneous demographic characteristics, such as age, family size, occupation, education. A given church may have just one target group. More frequently, however, it has two or more groups usually separated most easily on the basis of age.

Three examples of target groups would be people who prefer a great deal of experimentation in liturgy, those who like some experimentation, and those who are strict traditionalists. (Many other dimensions defining target groups might be considered; the experimental vs. traditional continuum was chosen for expositional purposes only.) In a very large church the needs of all three target groups could be met comfortably. In the small to medium-sized church, however, the needs of only one group might be satisfied.

The concepts of image and target groups definitions are closely connected. If a target group in a church is well defined, the church's image will often reflect characteristics of the target group. To the extent that the church's image is a clear reflection of the church's primary target group, it will attract other individuals who are either members of the target group already or who aspire to be members.

Several additional points about target groups should be made. First, target groups may be definable along several dimensions, e.g., traditionalism *and* sociability *and* the desire for church-affiliated programs. Second, church leaders should recognize that the congregation contains within it at least one and perhaps more than one identifiable target group. Third, the pastor should attempt to identify the target groups and their needs (here is where surveys and group meetings can be helpful). Fourth, the large church can (and probably should) attempt to design programs and liturgy to meet the needs of two or more target groups; small and medium-sized churches probably should not (they risk the danger of creating a diffuse image).

Differentiated Marketing

The strategy of differentiated marketing is closely related to the concept of target groups. A church employing this strategy designs marketing programs to meet the needs of the identifiable target group or groups it serves. If only one target group is served, the marketing program should be tailored to match the needs and characteristics of the group. For example, assume the profile of a target group is: (1) members have low-to-average education; (2) they have a fairly traditional outlook on life; and (3) they live in an area having only limited recreational facilities. To match this profile, the church's mass communications media (advertising, bulletins, and newsletters) should be composed using dignified but easily understandable language and construction; services should be somewhat conservative; and the church should sponsor as many recreational programs as resources permit.

If two or more distinct target groups are identifiable, the church should attempt to design a distinct marketing program for each group.

As an example of this idea, consider the needs of younger members of the congregation, particularly those in their late teens and early twenties. Based upon observation and comments we've heard from a number of clergy, it appears that the religious needs of this group are homogeneous but quite different from, say, the religious needs of those in their late twenties and older. Treating the whole congregation as if it had the same needs is not appreciated and frequently results in the departure of a large number of those in the disaffected group. Two distinct programs can better meet the needs of both groups and, if anything, increase internal harmony and satisfaction.

A number of recommendations have been presented for improving the marketing orientation of your church. Where you think the ideas are appropriate to your church's situation, put them to work. Do so with care and understanding, however, using an evolutionary rather than a revolutionary approach. As you move toward a marketing orientation, you will find guidance from the references listed in the Bibliography.

Chapter 6

Personnel Practices

Any manager's responsibility includes personnel matters, such as hiring, defining duties, compensation, and appraising employee performance. But these tasks often get short shrift in a church. An informal approach to personnel matters is often rationalized with the attitude that an organization with only one or a few paid staff people doesn't need a lot of personnel policies and procedures.

Having heard a number of ministers complain bitterly about the time and frustration involved in dealing with just one "difficult" church secretary, it seems eminently reasonable for churches to develop simple procedures to apply to paid staff members. The principles apply as well to part-time workers as they do to full-time personnel. The procedures outlined here should help you find and keep qualified staff people and cut down on job dissatisfaction and conflicts.

Hiring

When you have a position to be filled, several questions need exploration before you take any action:

1. What kind of candidate do we need?
2. How do we go about seeking candidates for the job?
3. How do we select the best candidate?
4. How can we avoid later misunderstandings between the new employee and the pastor or other supervisors?

To determine what kind of candidate you need, you should have a job description and a job specification. The job description will be discussed later in this chapter. The specification sets forth the knowledge, skills, and abilities required of an individual to perform competently in the job. For example, does the secretary need typing skills, knowledge of bookkeeping, a pleasant telephone voice and manner? An example of specifications for a representative job in a church is shown in Exhibit 6-1. Such specifications which describe the kind of person the church is seeking are helpful in both *recruiting* and *screening* candidates.

The job specification need not be developed in great detail, but it should represent mutual agreement by the pastor and the personnel committee. Otherwise there will be considerable opportunities for misunderstanding between the pastor and the committee (if both are involved in hiring) and between the pastor and the candidate who is hired. Misunderstanding may result in a mismatch, the hiring of a person who is not qualified for the job. When this happens, the cost in administrative time and effort gets very large.

To develop a job specification, you will need input from the lay board, the pastor, and any staff people directly concerned with the position to be filled. It is often useful to refer to job specifications for similar positions in businesses or other churches. A pitfall to be avoided is simply to describe the knowledge, skills, and abilities of the last incumbent in the job.

The job specification should be reasonably specific but not unduly restrictive. Treading this narrow line may take some discussion. A too lengthy list of requirements may screen out a desirable candidate; too vague a specification may make final selection very difficult.

With a job description and a job specification in hand you are ready to begin recruiting candidates.

Exhibit 6-1   Job Specification, Minister of Music

A. *Knowledge*
   1. Thorough, detailed knowledge of choral music techniques.
   2. Working knowledge of instrumental music.

    3. Understanding of church organizational structure and roles of key positions in that structure.

B. *Skills and Abilities*
    1. Enduring patience in working with volunteers.
    2. The ability to lead through persuasiveness and diplomacy at times or through authority and assertiveness when necessary.
    3. The ability to reach people with widely varying musical tastes while maintaining continuity in the program.
    4. The ability to teach.
    5. The ability to accompany instrumentally (extremely helpful though not essential).

C. *Personal Attributes*
    1. Conviction as to importance of music in the total church ministry.
    2. Willingness to yield personal desires to those of choir members when it is in the best interest of the church and the choir.
    3. Appreciation for widely varying musical styles.

Recruiting

Most church staffs are not large enough to have someone who can be transferred into a new job opening. However, if at all feasible, it is well to consider filling the vacant position with a member of the present staff, either as a promotion or as a means of broadening the person's skills. While selection of a present staff person may require additional training or modifying the job to fit the individual, these alternatives are much less expensive than recruiting someone from the outside.

Let's assume, however, that you will recruit from outside the organization. These are ways of finding job candidates:

    1. *Employment agencies.* A good one can do an excellent job of producing candidates and performing preliminary screening for you against your job description and specification. The agency will not charge you for this service, but your eventual candidate may negotiate to have you pay the agency fee.
    2. *Advertising in the local newspapers.* When you place a classified ad, you act as your own employment agency. You

can request "resumés only" to avoid unnecessary interviewing. Use the resumés for the initial screening. Screening interviews can be shared between the pastor and the personnel committee. If you use the job description and specification, everyone helping with the screening interviews will have the same understanding of what kind of person is needed to fill the job.

3. *The broadcast approach.* Spreading the word that you have a job vacancy to the governing board, church committees, and the congregation as a whole will turn up a number of names. It may also turn up some new headaches in that church members will recommend their sisters, aunts, and friends. Sometimes the major qualifications of these candidates are that they "need the job." Your job description and specification can help you deal tactfully with these well-intentioned recommendations.

What about the issue of hiring a church member for a nonpastoral job in the church? One consideration is that of "taking care of our own." Another is the issue of getting the job done efficiently. A third, and perhaps most important from our discussions with pastors, is the problem of the church member staff person whose concern for the church and its fellowship gets in the way of carrying out his or her duties in an unbiased manner. In other words, the church administration is frequently better served by hiring nonmember staff persons.

Selecting the Best Candidate

Now you are ready to screen resumés and hold preliminary interviews. No matter how it is done, the screening process is time consuming. The only way to speed it up is to give it high priority with the pastor and others who will be involved in interviewing, but you can make the process more efficient by either of these methods:

1. The pastor conducts interviews until he or she has identified two or three good candidates. These are referred to the personnel committee for its appraisal.

2. The personnel committee does the screening interviews and presents the two or three best candidates for the pastor's appraisal.

A third approach is to have the pastor and the committee

interview all candidates. This is very time consuming and tends to be used when there is no job description and specification as a means of making sure that everyone is satisfied.

Certainly if the employee is going to be working for the pastor, the pastor must do the final interviewing and make the final decision.

What if the recruiting process turns up a "super" person whom all concerned would like to have on board but who doesn't really fit the specifications? This can and does happen and presents a real dilemma. Before you make a hiring decision, consider what the impact will be on the rest of the staff organization and how other jobs might have to be restructured in light of the decision.

A search for job candidates can be seen as an opportunity for enhancing the public relations efforts of the church. An advertisement or circular for the job is a chance to "sell the church." Competent interviewing, use of job descriptions and specifications, and prompt and courteous communications with candidates all give the impression of a well-managed church. Communications with candidates must, of course, include notifying unsuccessful candidates as soon as the decision about them has been made. A thoughtful letter is preferable to leaving it up to the candidate to call in and be told that he or she is no longer in the running.

Avoiding Misunderstandings Later On

At the point of hiring a good manager makes sure the candidate has a clear understanding of certain basics of the job, including pay, policy on granting raises, fringe benefits, duties, authority, responsibility, relationships with others in the organization, hours, and working facilities and conditions.

The pastor or other administrator must anticipate the kinds of questions a prospective employee will have and be prepared to provide answers. This means explaining existing policies and being clear about areas not covered by policy. Questions like these may be expected:

1. How soon before I can expect a raise? How much of a raise is customary?
2. Are there duties I am expected to perform that are not spelled out in my job description?
3. How will my performance be evaluated? How often? By whom?

The agreements reached at the time of hiring can be spelled out in the form of a commitment by both parties. A written agreement of this type is shown in Exhibit 6-2.

Exhibit 6-2*

October 20, 1973

Mrs. John R. Shipwash
1940 Brantley Street
Winston-Salem, North Carolina 27103

Dear Joyce:

I am pleased that you have agreed to accept employment as our Parish Secretary, and I look forward to working with you. What follows is a summation of the things we talked about which are relevant to this position. After you have read it carefully, please either sign the original and return it to me for our parish files, or call me for an appointment to discuss some possible alterations.

JOB DESCRIPTION

As Parish Secretary you will be expected to provide complete secretarial services to the Rector and to the general parish (which, from time to time, will include non-parochial organizations such as Brownies and Girl Scouts). In addition to general stenographic and typing services, filing, and general office records maintenance, you will be expected to post the pledge cards each week, count and deposit the Sunday collection, send out statements, write all checks, keep all financial records accurate and up-to-date, and make monthly reports to the Vestry concerning our financial condition. You shall also be responsible for the reproduction and mailing of all printed matter relating to parish activities. Among your more important special activities will be the preparation of a parish directory each August and the preparation of the annual parochial report during the first week in January.

Although you are technically employed by the Vestry and paid by the Vestry through an appropriation of necessary funds, your work will be supervised by me as Rector of the parish. I will represent

---

*Reprinted with permission, St. Timothy's Episcopal Church, Winston-Salem, North Carolina.

your interests and needs to the Vestry, assist you in acquiring and maintaining necessary office equipment, and will be of general assistance whenever possible.

WORK SCHEDULE

You will be expected to work in the parish office from 8 a.m. until noon and from 1 p.m. until 5 p.m. each week Mondays through Fridays.

SALARY ADMINISTRATION

As we agreed, your starting salary shall be $. Your salary will be reviewed annually by the Finance and Personnel Committees and recommended changes will be included in the proposed budget for the following year. All changes in the parish secretary's salary must be approved by a majority vote of the Vestry. One-twelfth of the annual salary, less State and Federal Withholding, shall be paid to you each month. No deductions are made for Social Security or for any other type of retirement plan.

ABSENCE FROM REGULAR DUTIES

The Parish Secretary shall receive with pay the following holidays: New Year's Day, Independence Day, Labor Day, Thanksgiving Day, Christmas (one and one-half days) and Easter (one and one-half days).

In the first year of your employment, you will receive a paid vacation of one week. After the first year, the vacation period shall be extended to two weeks. Such vacation normally shall be taken during the summer months (June through August) but may, with adequate arrangements to cover the needs of the office, be taken otherwise if necessary. The two weeks may be taken together or separately, but any schedule must be agreed upon by the Rector.

Absence of the Parish Secretary due to either sickness or accident for a period up to and including one month shall require no adjustment in salary. Absence beyond one month shall require that the normal salary be made available for any necessary and temporary replacement. Normally, employment shall be terminated at age 65. Employment may be continued, however, by an annual review which indicates acceptable performance can be maintained for the ensuing year.

Should you wish to resign prior to age 65, a one month notice shall be given to the Rector when possible, and the Rector will furnish letters of recommendation to prospective employers. In the event involuntary termination seems desirable, the Personnel Committee shall review the matter with the Rector and with the Parish Secretary, and if determined advisable, the Senior Warden, on behalf of the Vestry, shall terminate employment with severance pay in the amount of one-half of one month's salary.

Very truly yours,

John R. Campbell
Rector

JRC:mc

DATE:_____

I understand and agree to the conditions of employment as stated above.

(Signed)_____

(Date)_____

Compensation

Church employees are no different from any other employees in their attitudes toward compensation. They want to be paid what they believe the job to be worth, and they want recognition in their paycheck for good performance on the job.

Regardless of the size of your paid staff, these should be your objectives in compensation policy:

1. Compensation should be based on the value of the job to the church.
2. Compensation should be in reasonable relationship to the value of a similar job in other organizations in the area.
3. The job should be valued fairly in relationship to other paid positions in the church.

If you can meet these objectives, you will keep disappointments and friction over salaries to a minimum.

Most organizations set minimum and maximum salaries for each job category. This is good policy for churches, too. The technique for setting appropriate salary ranges is called job evaluation. It is used by most companies today to meet the compensation objectives outlined above. Essentially it involves these steps:

1. Identifying the different jobs in the organization and preparing job descriptions for each. (Examples of job descriptions are shown in Exhibit 6-3.)
2. Comparing the value of each job against an objective set of criteria. These criteria, or yardsticks, for evaluating the relative worth of jobs are the technical component of a job evaluation system and will not be described here. You will be able to find in your community a well-managed company which has a job evaluation plan which can be made available to you to evaluate the few jobs on the church staff. The company's personnel manager can be a valuable resource in applying evaluation criteria to your jobs.
3. Determining the salaries for comparable jobs in other organizations in your community. Salary surveys are done in almost every community, usually by the larger employers, and these surveys can be made available to you. Don't be too concerned that church jobs are "different." This is not an insurmountable problem.
4. Evaluating jobs to establish salary ranges. The ranges you establish should represent fair relationships between the jobs in your church and with salaries paid on the outside. Once developed, salary ranges are kept up-to-date by annual review against the community salary survey data. A personnel manager in the congregation can guide this relatively simple checking process.

Some ministers wonder whether it is necessary for a small church with only a few salaried positions to go through the process of job evaluation. You don't have to do it, of course, but you do have to deal with employees who want a reasonable explanation of why they are being paid what they are being paid. Job evaluation techniques make it possible for you to have a rational discussion based on facts, not feelings. Job evaluation is a tool for avoiding salary conflicts.

Once the initial task of fitting the current jobs into an evaluation pattern has been done, it is relatively easy to fit changed jobs into the system. We are finding that an increasing number of small churches are using this tool, and most large churches have been doing it for some years.

Developing Job Descriptions

We have discussed the usefulness of job descriptions in hiring employees and in determining fair compensation. (Developing a job description for the pastor is discussed in detail in chapter 1. The value of the job descriptions for volunteer jobs is presented in chapter 7.) How do you go about developing job descriptions (the process of "job analysis")?

1. The pastor and the staff employees, usually together with the personnel committee, sit down and talk about the desirability of having job descriptions.
2. Each employee is asked to write a description of his or her own job, using no more than a couple of pages. It is helpful to suggest that the employee include the priority of the various tasks, the percentage of his or her time spent on each duty or group of duties, any special skills needed (such as operating equipment), complexity of decisions required, and the relationship of this job to others in the church.

Either the pastor or a member of the personnel committee should review the employee statements and prepare job descriptions from them. The pastor or committee member should ask questions to resolve any issues that are not clear and prepare a one or one and one-half page description which includes the following elements:

1. A brief statement of the purpose of the job (why it exists). In Exhibit 6-3 (at the end of the chapter) the statement is headed "Principal Function."
2. A list of the key duties or responsibilities of the job.
3. Statements to highlight key responsibilities, such as approvals for expenditures or special skills required.
4. A final statement such as "performs other duties as requested" is useful to avoid resentment when an employee is asked to perform minor tasks.

Job descriptions should be reviewed each time an employee's performance is reviewed. The employee and the pastor, or other supervisor, agree on changes to the job description at that time.[1]

[1]Excellent additional detail on job analysis is found in William F. Glueck, *Personnel: A Diagnostic Approach*, rev. ed. (Dallas, Tex.: Business Publications, Inc., 1978).

Salary Administration

Salary administration encompasses pay increases and payroll cost control. The three significant policy areas are: granting raises, progression of an employee's salary within the salary range, and fringe benefits.

Employees need to know, at least in approximate terms, how often they will be reviewed for salary adjustments and what kind of raise is reasonable to expect. This should be spelled out at the time of hiring. Decisions on these policies would normally be reached with the personnel committee after checking the practices of other organizations in the community.

In today's inflationary environment, policy on raises is changing radically. In profit-making organizations an annual raise of about 7 percent to 10 percent was customary until recently. Today with the cost of living going up at the rate of 10 to 12 percent a year, a 10 percent or 12 percent raise just keeps the employee even. It doesn't represent salary progress.

Companies are dealing with this problem by holding more frequent salary reviews, adding merit increases on top of cost-of-living raises, giving bonuses for meritorious performances (to avoid building these one-shot payments into the basic salary structure), and reviewing the job evaluation system at least once a year to make sure the salaries they are paying are in line with community averages.

Raises should be budgeted, a point which seems obvious but is often overlooked in organizations with few employees. What usually happens is a last-minute, year-end debate on "what do we have to give Betty to keep her from leaving?", with one eye on the stewardship campaign and the other on the deficit and little or no regard for established procedures and policies. Building planned and realistic raises into the budget enables award of pay increases at the appropriate time in relation to employee performance, length of service, the findings of community salary surveys, and other pertinent information.

To help budget salary increases, let's take a closer look at the salary range:

1. *Minimum and maximum*. If an employee is doing the job, he or she should be paid at least the minimum of the range. An

employee should not receive more than the maximum for the job with some rare exceptions, the principal one being extended length of service in the same job. In this case it may be desirable to award a "length of service increase," which is recognized as being above the maximum and is awarded only to that particular employee, not to any occupant of that job. Normally an employee who is above the maximum established for the job is not entitled to a merit increase.

2. *Midpoint of the range.* In conventional salary practice employees tend to move from minimum to midpoint by means of automatic or semiautomatic raises, often at yearly intervals. Beyond the midpoint they move on a merit basis only.

3. *Movement of the range itself.* The salary range will be shifted upward if a community salary survey indicates the need. Normally ranges for the several jobs in the church organization will move proportionately upward at the same time so that the relationship between the jobs, as established by the job evaluation procedure, will not be altered.

Policy on fringe benefits usually stems from the policy of the denomination, sometimes tempered by community practices. Also the financial situation of the particular church will influence its own policy on fringes provided to employees. Unfortunately, the small size of church staffs often hinders churches from providing some of the benefits enjoyed by larger organizations. Nonetheless, the normal employee relations criteria of fairness, social responsibility, and motivation of good performance need to be recognized in making decisions on the fringe benefits package. From the point of view of administrative effectiveness it is hard to defend a practice of substandard or nonexistent fringes to the church's paid personnel.

The subject of pensions particularly warrants scrutiny. A number of denominations have pension plans available for both lay and clergy employees. Where these are not available, a church, particularly a small one, may think they cannot afford to establish a pension policy or fund. As the pastor, church secretary, or music director grows old in the church's service, the problem becomes more acute until the crisis time is reached. Then crisis measures must be taken, and these measures often fail to meet the real need. Just as a banker counsels clients to think ahead and save for their children's education, so the personnel committee must plan ahead for the retirement of key people. Deferring action on reserves for a pension can be more harmful than deferring maintenance on the roof of the church.

Appraising Employee Performance

There are three reasons for appraising an employee's performance:

1. To decide about awarding a raise.
2. To motivate improved performance on the present job.
3. To prepare and guide an employee for promotion. (While there are relatively few opportunities for promotion within a typical church organization, your employees may well be looking beyond the church for career opportunities. Using performance appraisal to provide guidance in career planning can be helpful to the employee.)

Techniques for conducting employee appraisals fall generally into two categories:

1. *Merit rating* is a conventional approach using standardized forms that list a number of factors on which the employee's performance is graded. An example of a merit rating form is shown in Exhibit 6-4 (at the end of the chapter). Personnel managers on your personnel committee can provide details on forms they have used with success. Suffice it to say that merit rating is used primarily for compensation decisions. It is used, to a limited extent, to stimulate improved performance by calling attention to factors on which the employee is judged to do well or poorly.

   There is considerable agreement today that merit rating has limited usefulness in actually motivating employees to do a better job. Research indicates that criticism of performance is not a motivating influence and that praise, though it may be heartwarming, motivates at a decreasing rate.
2. *Appraising against job-related standards* is a technique that many companies are using now. (Chapter 1, in a discussion on appraising the pastor's performance, provides a related approach to performance appraisal but with an annual review because of the pastor/board relationship.) Also called "management by objectives" (MBO), the technique can be applied in church organizations this way:

a) The pastor or other supervisor sits down with each employee to agree on targets for programs, tasks, and other activities for the period ahead. One target may be set for a task to be completed in three weeks, another in three months, another at the end of the year. Exhibit 6-5 (at the end of the chapter) provides a simple form for recording the information discussed.

b) When the time for meeting the target arrives, the supervisor and employee sit down to review performance on the task and discuss its accomplishment. They then set new tasks and new target dates.

c) At salary review time the record of task accomplishments becomes the basis for the decision about whether to award a raise and how much of an increase is appropriate.

This approach has the merit of being objective because it is job related. A major motivational factor is that the employee is involved in setting his or her own targets.

The use of MBO techniques need not be limited to large, bureaucratic organizations. Our discussions with pastors indicate increasing interest in making use of these techniques in large and small churches.[2]

Research in the complex field of motivating employees by means of performance appraisals shows that salary should not be discussed at the same time as issues of improving performance.[3] The reason is that if an employee knows that salary will be a topic of the discussion, he or she will be listening only for the "magic words." He or she won't be paying much attention to what you have to say about doing a better job.

The proper approach, then, is to plan one discussion on better job performance and another one, at a different time, on the subject of the employee's raise. When the management-by-objectives approach is followed, discussions on targets and job performance are held frequently, not just once a year. Frequent job performance reviews have far more motivational value than annual appraisals.

---

[2]For more detail see Harold D. Koontz, *Appraising Managers As Managers* (New York: McGraw-Hill, Inc., 1971).
[3]See "Split Roles in Performance Appraisal" by Meyer *et al.*, *Harvard Business Review* (January-February, 1965).

Personnel Records

Churches' personnel records, like those of many small organizations, tend to be sketchy and may not even meet legal requirements. At a minimum the church should maintain a file for each employee containing the original records of hiring, a history of salary adjustments, and copies of appraisals.

Current job descriptions and job specifications should be filed, and there should be records of transactions covered by the fringe benefit program.

Exhibit 6-3a

Job Description: Associate Pastor for Adult Ministries*

Principal function:

The Associate Pastor shall assist the pastor in the care and oversight of the church membership. He shall give direction, leadership, and oversight to all adult and college ministries.

Responsibilities:

1. Assist the pastor in pastoral ministries as requested.

2. Coordinate all adult educational and training ministries, including personal ministry to departmental leaders.

3. Coordinate all college, educational, and training ministries and lead in personal discipleship among college students.

4. Lead and coordinate all training ministries of the church, including Church Training and the Christian Education Institute.

5. He shall serve as staff liaison for, and work with, the following committees:

---

*The job descriptions in Exhibits 6-3-*a* through 6-3*g* are reprinted with the permission of Calvary Baptist Church of Winston-Salem, North Carolina. These represent the staffing of a large church in order to provide the reader with a useful spectrum of job descriptions. Smaller churches can combine "responsibilities" statements from several of the descriptions to compose drafts pertinent to their smaller staffs.

6. He shall give leadership to the adult work sub-committee of the nominating committee.

7. He shall have oversight of all formal discipling ministries of the church.

8. His weekly duties include prayer and study, teaching, prospect and membership visitation, counseling and administration.

Exhibit 6-3b

Job Description: Assistant Pastor for Children's Ministries

Principal Function:
The Assistant Pastor for Children's Ministries shall assist the pastor in the care and oversight of the church membership. He shall give specific oversight to the children's ministries of the church.

Responsibilities:
1. Assist the pastor in pastoral ministries as requested.

2. Coordinate all children's educational and training ministries, including personal ministry to children's departmental leaders and workers, and pastoral ministry to children within those departments.

3. He shall serve as Assistant Principal for the Day School and shall be responsible for the day to day operation of the school and the oversight of the faculty and the School Coordinator.

4. He shall plan and execute all children's camps, retreats, and Vacation Bible Schools with a view toward winning children to Christ and nurturing them in the faith.

5. He shall direct summer day ministries to children and summer children's outreach ministries, such as backyard Bible clubs.

6. He shall serve as staff liaison and work with the following committees: Nursery, Baptismal, Kindergarten and Day School.

7. His weekly duties include prayer and study, teaching, prospect and membership visitation, counselling and administration.

Exhibit 6-3c

Job Description: Assistant Pastor for Youth Ministries

Principal Function:

The Assistant Pastor for Youth Ministries shall assist the pastor in the care and oversight of the church membership. He shall have specific responsibility for the oversight of all youth ministries of the church.

Responsibilities:

1. Assist the pastor in pastoral ministries as requested.
2. Coordinate all youth educational training and outreach ministries, including personal ministry to youth departmental leaders, and pastoral ministries to the youth in those departments.
3. He shall plan and execute all youth camps and retreats and seminars with a view to evangelism and discipleship.
4. He shall serve as staff liaison for, and work with, the following committees:

5. He shall give leadership to the youth work sub-committee of the nominating committee.
6. His weekly duties include prayer and study, teaching, prospect and membership visitation, counseling, high school and junior high school campus contacts, discipling growth groups, leadership to evangelistic and visitation outreach, and administration.

Exhibit 6-3d

Job Description: Minister of Music

Principal Function:
The Minister of Music shall give leadership to a comprehensive church music ministry.

Responsibilities:
1. Assist the pastor in planning the order of service for all public worship of the church.
2. Lead and train musical groups and lead congregational singing for all stated and special public worship services.
3. Have administrative responsibilities for the organist and pianist and their necessary replacements.
4. Have spiritual concern for and ministry to all members involved in the music ministry.
5. Plan and execute outreach music ministries, including music specials, both within and without the church building.
6. Supervise the maintenance of, and plan additions to, the church music library, musical equipment, and instruments for use in the church program.
7. Serve as staff liaison for, and work with, the following committees:

8. He shall assist in special administrative tasks as assigned by the pastor.
9. His weekly duties include: leading in public worship, choir rehearsal, visitation, and ministry to those in the music program, administration, prospect and membership visitation, and prayer and Bible study for his own personal and spiritual growth.

Exhibit 6-3e

Job Description: Business Administrator

Principal Function:
The business administrator shall develop and administer policies for carrying out office activity, custodial work, financial administration, and church publications.

Responsibilities:

1. Oversee secretarial schedules, approve work flow, approve and schedule absences, vacations, personal leave, enforcing Personnel Manual, providing resources for secretarial staff, evaluating performance, serving as communication link with Personnel Committee, and having power to hire and fire in counsel with the Personnel Committee and Pastor.

2. Oversee Custodial and Maintenance Staff, approving and maintaining work schedules, approving and scheduling absences, vacations, personal leave, enforcing the Personnel Manual, evaluating performance, serving as communication link with the Personnel Committee and having power to hire and fire in counsel with the Personnel Committee and Pastor. (In both cases, Nos. 1 and 2, the phrase "in counsel with the Personnel Committee and Pastor" shall mean he may initiate hiring and firing, keeping both the Committee and the Pastor aware of need for such action and counseling with them prior to such action where reasonable. Hiring and firing are both done more judiciously where the knowledge and consent of appropriate responsible groups are gained in advance.)

3. Oversee maintenance of all financial records by the Financial Secretary, organizing the office, overseeing the bond program, maintaining repayment schedules, maintaining insurance programs, overseeing permanent records of the church, financial reports, approving expenditures, certifying authorizations of Payment Approval Forms, and serving as staff resource person to the Finance Committee.

4. In a general sense, assist the Pastor in overseeing work of lay committees. A Deacon and a Staff member are normally

assigned to each Committee to give leadership to each Committee, and to guarantee integration of the individual Committee's work with the entire ministry.

5. Editing "Visitor," the weekly newspaper, the "Lamplighter," the Wednesday evening publication, a prospective television monthly mailout, monthly sermon printing, and overseeing the tape ministry.

Exhibit 6-3f

Job Description: Church and Pastor's Secretary

Principal Function: The church and pastor's secretary is to provide office service for the pastor and to maintain church publications, and records.

Responsibilities:

1. Type the pastor's sermons and correspondence.
2. Maintain the pastor's and church schedule and serve as receptionist for the pastor.
3. Prepare church-wide mailings including "The Weekly Visitor," "Lamplighter," and general mailings.
4. Maintain church membership, including baptismal files and records, and the pastor's files.
5. Provide secretarial services for special projects, pastor's class, baptismal services, and committees directly related to the pastor's work.
6. Receive and sort the pastor's mail.

Exhibit 6-3g

Job Description: Evangelism Secretary

Principal Function: The evangelism secretary is to provide coordination for the evangelism training ministry and visitation program.

Responsibilities:

1. Maintain general prospect files from visitors' cards and other sources.

2. Provide and maintain evangelism manuals and prepare weekly visits for those enrolled in the evangelism training program.

3. Order and maintain usable supplies of all evangelism materials including tracts, follow-up materials, Scripture portions for distribution.

4. Provide secretarial services for all evangelistic, outreach, and discipleship programs of the church.

5. Prepare weekly mailings to visitors in public services, and maintain visitors' records.

6. Maintain all correspondence for radio and television ministries including gift offers.

Exhibit 6-3h

Job Description: Financial Secretary

Principal Function: The financial secretary is to maintain all church financial records and business files.

Responsibilities:

1. Weekly recording of personal contributions and preparation and mailing of annual individual statements of giving.

2. Preparation of monthly, quarterly, and annual financial statements.

3. Post receipts and disbursements of all accounts according to the financial system and current policy.

4. Prepare bank reconciliation statements monthly.

5. Make appropriate monthly, quarterly and annual governmental tax reports.

6. Maintain up-to-date bond registrars, and reconcile bond and interest payments for all church bond programs.

7. Prepare and issue checks according to church policy.

8. Receive and answer all questions concerning financial matters, maintaining a file of invoices, correspondence and reports.

9. Participate in other office duties as needed and assigned.

Exhibit 6-3i

Job Description: Receptionist and Records Secretary

Principal Function: The receptionist and records secretary shall take all telephone calls and greet all visitors to the church office. She shall maintain appropriate educational records for all divisions.

Responsibilities:

1. Answer and appropriately process all telephone calls and messages to the church office.

2. Receive and appropriately refer all visitors to the church offices.

3. Sort and classify all mail; receive and appropriately refer all deliveries to the church office.

4. Maintain the general church calendar for reference.

5. Take reservations for church functions, such as special meals and regular fellowship suppers.

6. Maintain Sunday School enrollment cards, including the processing for Sunday School of new members.

7. Type miscellaneous items as directed and assist with general office projects as needed.

Exhibit 6-3j

Job Description: Church Custodian

Principal Function: The church custodian shall see that church property is in a state of readiness for appropriate use at all times.

Responsibilities:

1. Maintain the auditorium for all public worship.
2. Clean offices and school classrooms daily for use.
3. Maintain the fellowship hall for use as assigned.
4. Maintain clean restrooms and see that all restrooms are supplied as necessary.
5. Prepare the auditorium and chapel for weddings, funerals, and special meetings.
6. Move deliveries to proper storage.
7. Operate heating and cooling equipment according to schedule.
8. Prepare baptistry as directed and clean properly following use.
9. Maintain cleaning schedule for walls, windows, carpets, and floors.
10. Open the building each morning and prepare it for use as scheduled.
11. Arranging furniture in school classrooms on weekly basis as scheduled.
12. Mowing and trimming grass and shrubbery around immediate edge of building in cooperation with the Properties Committee weekly schedule.
13. Perform other responsibilities as assigned.

Exhibit 6-4

Typical graphic rating scale*

		Out-standing	Good	Satis-factory	Fair	Unsat-isfac-tory
Quantity of work Volume of acceptable work under normal conditions Comments:		☐	☐	☐	☐	☐
Quality of work Thoroughness, neatness and accuracy of work Comments:		☐	☐	☐	☐	☐
Knowledge of job Clear understanding of the facts or factors pertinent to the job Comments:		☐	☐	☐	☐	☐
Personal qualities Personality, appearance, sociability, leadership, integrity Comments:		☐	☐	☐	☐	☐
Cooperation Ability and willingness to work with associates, supervisors, and subordinates toward common goals Comments:		☐	☐	☐	☐	☐

Name_____ Dept._____ Date_____

*Reproduced with permission from William Glueck, *Personnel: A Diagnostic Approach,* rev. ed. (Dallas, Tex.: Business Publications, Inc., 1978), p. 302. ©1978 by Business Publications, Inc.

Dependability ☐ ☐ ☐ ☐ ☐
Conscientious, thor-
ough, accurate, reliable
with respect to atten-
dance, lunch periods,
reliefs, etc.
Comments:

Initiative ☐ ☐ ☐ ☐ ☐
Earnestness in seeking
increased responsibili-
ties. Self-starting, una-
fraid to proceed alone?
Comments:

Exhibit 6-5

GOAL-SETTING APPRAISAL FORM*

This form may be used for either an individual or a group.

Your Goals		Attainment Steps	Solutions	Expected Benefits		Progress Report
First Goal: Enter only one goal in this space.	Target date	What work activities are necessary to achieve this goal?	I will successfully achieve this step by:	How will the organization and I benefit from this achievement?	Evaluation date	Present standing and standing on each evaluation date.
Second Goal: Enter only one goal in this space.						
Third Goal: Enter only one goal in this space.						

*Richard Henderson, *Compensation Management* (Reston, Va.: Reston Publishing Company, Inc., a Prentice-Hall Company, 11480 Sunset Hills Road, Reston, Va.). Reprinted with permission.

Chapter 7

Management of Expectations Within Your Church

A church often finds its spiritual mission grounded in secular realities. Budgets must be balanced; volunteer workers must be managed, and occasional arguments must be arbitrated. These problems are complicated because congregations and their pastors often accept more programs and activities than they have resources to accommodate. To satisfy these extensive work requirements, the church must rely heavily on the talents of inexperienced part-time and volunteer employees.

As the paid professional leader of the church, the pastor is held responsible for the effective resolution of church problems and the successful accomplishment of church projects. Yet as noted in chapter 1, rarely are a pastor's responsibilities clearly defined or the ramifications of these responsibilities completely understood by the congregation. Instead the pastor is viewed as that person who is held accountable for things "going well." The pastor must constantly offer inspiring sermons, thus encouraging membership to grow while keeping a careful watch on budgetary considerations.

It is imperative that the pastor recognize these dual roles and accept the potential for conflict inherent in them. Expectations associated with the managerial aspects of a pastor's job may not always completely agree with the value and expectations of that individual who has answered the call to be a pastor. Spiritual objectives are often restrained by secular inefficiencies.

A church is an organization, and, as such, its goals can be attained only through maximizing all of its resources, including its people.

This responsibility falls upon the pastor who must manage the human resources of the congregation effectively.

Ironically, the same individual who feels called to influence the members of the congregation in respect to matters of faith may feel very reticent about shaping the behavior of others in respect to mundane matters, such as getting bills paid on time or mediating a dispute between employees and volunteers. Such problems are typical, however, and must be handled with understanding and skill if a church and its pastor are to prosper. More than one pastor who served in the pulpit with grace has lost the church because of an unwillingness or failure to manage it well.

A widely accepted definition of management is that it consists of getting things done through other people. In order to delegate responsibility successfully and motivate others, a manager must first aspire to understand himself or herself better. Implicit in this view is the recognition that one needs to be able to manage one's self well before one can be an effective manager of others.

Today's pastor is likely to be well ahead of the average business manager in exposure to concepts from the behavioral sciences, either by professional training or as a result of constant reading. This chapter and the one that follows it are intended to build on this knowledge. Brief descriptions and explanations of theories related to the concept of role, motivation, authority and power, and the dynamics of human interaction are interspersed in these chapters with examples as to how a pastor or other church leaders may find these behavioral theories useful in managing the human resources of the church.

This chapter emphasizes role theory as a useful vehicle for clarifying expectations in organizational life. Chapter 8 is intended to serve as a primer on the sources and dynamics of a pastor's influence. Once the pastor clarifies his or her own role and those of the people who work with him or her, chapter 8 should increase his or her ability to get things done through the regular staff and volunteers from the congregation.

Role Theory

Everyone has seen, and some people have participated in, television or theatrical roles. In this sense we are accustomed to acting out a role. It is often startling to the instructor who uses role plays in classroom training to see how well people project themselves into situations they know little about. People are able to "get into role" with considerable facility because they are constantly on stage. In short, we human beings are accustomed to role playing and know the main rules of behavior that go with a large number of roles. As with so many aspects of our reality, such ability and knowledge can be advantageous but also troublesome.

For example, upon meeting a minister, a person is likely to know the general scope of the minister's work and some of the specific things that are included. Such knowledge cues the person to react within appropriate guidelines when in the pastor's presence. In like fashion the minister's awareness of the attitudes and behaviors expected of the role permit, and also constrain, him or her to fulfill the expectations of the person. Thus preconceived notions of the minister's role affect both the "occupant's" (minister) and the "sender's" expected reactions. The model is not only *interactive* but is also *dynamic,* as role senders seek to influence the occupant's behavior by subtle suggestion as to whether they approve or disapprove of the occupant's attitude toward the role and his or her actions within it.

Overall the sets of expectations that comprise roles act both to allocate the functions served by individuals within our society and to contribute to a degree of predictability and stability in human relationships. Although these functions are obviously useful, being the occupant of a particular role can often be as stressful as it is satisfying.

The illustration presented in Exhibit 7-1 graphically conveys the pressures which are apt to be experienced by the individual whose professional role is that of pastor. Obviously a pastor has a lot of different "role senders," and the expectations which they convey are not necessarily consistent. Any time this many role senders converge on an occupant, role conflicts occur and the occupant experiences stress. Let's examine the specific reasons for such role-related stress.

Intrasender Conflict

The expectations sent by any single role sender are not always internally consistent. For example, the senior member of the board might let the pastor know that he expects him to increase both the number and average amount of members' pledges yet leads the pastor to understand that he must do this without talking frankly about the church's need for money.

Intersender Conflict

The various people with whom a role occupant interacts regularly have a way of "sending" different expectations as to how one should conduct oneself and even how one ought to feel in respect to it—they disagree, knowingly or unknowingly, about the content and performance of the role. To illustrate: Some of the pastor's congregation may think that the pastor ought to abstain from social activism; others will hold that his or her ministry ought to involve being "on the barricades" of social change as some ministers were during the late 1960s.

Exhibit 7-1

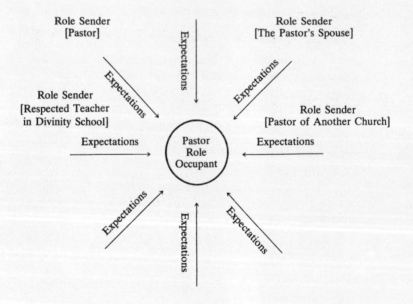

Role Sender
[Chairman, Church Board]

Role Sender
[Pastor]

Role Sender
[The Pastor's Spouse]

Role Sender
[Respected Teacher
in Divinity School]

Role Sender
[Pastor of Another Church]

Expectations

Pastor
Role
Occupant

Expectations

Role Sender
[A Young Member]

Role Sender
[An Elderly Member]

Role Sender
[A Minority Member]

Person-Role Conflicts

The occupant has his or her own concept of the role and how one ought to conduct oneself within it. Thus one is a major "sender" of expectations to oneself and will frequently be more critical than others of one's failure to meet these expectations.

Role Overload

The diversity and sheer weight of what the occupant of a role would have to do to meet all of the expectations "sent" to him or her may be too great—especially over an extended period of time. A "no-win" situation develops from the classic problem of taking on more tasks than can possibly be accomplished.

Multiple Roles

In addition to pastor, an individual may serve many other roles (i.e., spouse, friend, parent). Each of these roles carries with it associated expectations that may conflict with the obligations sent and received in one's other roles.

Suggested Applications of Role Theory

Pastor-managers can use the framework of role theory to gain increased understanding of their relationship with and participation in their environment. An increased awareness of diverse role expectations may lead to new personal and managerial insights. Role conflicts and inconsistencies can be anticipated, thus allowing pastors to accept some of them, reject others, and renegotiate still others. This approach to clarifying their place in their environment has distinct managerial overtones as it provides an orderly way of identifying and considering problems to which there would appear to be very little structure.

Pastors who apply role theory analysis to their position may encounter difficulties weighing each individual's expectations. The appropriate response to this state of affairs, managerially and otherwise, is to seek to clarify and rank these obligations. If, for example, there is no written job description (or position description) for the position of pastor, it would make sense to develop one. A methodology for doing this is presented in chapters 1 and 6.

This same approach, or a modified version of it, may be applied to other full-time, part-time, or volunteer roles. Almost everyone appreciates knowing what is expected of one, preferably before one becomes involved with an organization but certainly as an ongoing guide to one's efforts to contribute to it.

Role Problems with Church Employees

Although it is usually the church secretary who suffers most from excessive and conflicting role expectations, other paid members of the staff may also feel confusion and frustration. Such lack of role clarity is fertile soil for conflicts among paid staff members and volunteers. Confusion over job responsibilities leads to a lack of coordination, to duplications of effort, and to perceived invasions of territories that individual members of the staff believe, rightly or wrongly, to be theirs. The pastor is also likely to encounter problems when he or she needs to replace or add staff members if there is not a precise mapping of current responsibilities within the church.

Job Descriptions Plus Continuing Communication

The development of job descriptions is an iterative process. As the needs of the church change, the pool of skills and talent also changes with departures and arrivals, and various members of the staff need new challenges to promote their growth and keep them at their best. This is not to say that the pastor and staff spend part of every week working with one another on clarifying their roles. The point is that there needs to be reasonably frequent communication to assess and revise positional expectations. Job descriptions should be reviewed by the pastor and with individual members of the staff *at least* once a year and more frequently if the church organization is undergoing significant changes. While complete knowledge and agreement among the pastor and staff members on individual responsibilities and organizational territory are elusive goals, working in this direction will promote the effective functioning of the church. (See chapter 6 for more discussion of job descriptions and performance appraisals.)

Role Problems with Volunteers

Volunteer members of the church staff and committee structure tend to be a mixed blessing. The attitude of some individuals who offer their services without pay is that this gives them license to establish their own rules or expectations for whatever function they are performing. At the same time the pastor or church administrator often feels that he or she has no real leverage for dealing with volunteers who exceed their boundaries or fail to meet expectations. After all, how can you fire someone who is not a paid employee? The leader's discomfort in this type of situation is exacerbated if the volunteer is a relative or an influential member of the congregation and community. In role theory terms the leader's indecision in dealing with such a person may reflect his or her confusion over the respective roles of each. Is the person a subordinate, a parishioner, or, in effect, one of his or her bosses? Realistically the volunteer may be all three—especially if the pastor reinforces the volunteer's perception that this is the case.

Using Job Descriptions with Volunteers to Promote Understanding, Agreement, and Commitment to Their Roles

It may come as a surprise to some pastors and church leaders that the use of job descriptions is a growing practice in organizations that rely heavily upon volunteer services. The practice has several distinct benefits. First, the existence of a job description for a volunteer position is both an instrument of communication and a type of contact. Properly written, the description conveys the importance of the role to the church, its boundaries, and the expectations of the individual who accepts it. Second, by discussing the description with the volunteer, the pastor or other church leader may establish, either explicitly or implicitly, a commitment on the part of the individual to work within the guidelines of the description and to meet the expectations conveyed by it.

Should the volunteer not work out, then the job description provides a fairly solid basis for discussing whatever these problems might mean.

As with regular employees, such a discussion might result in any number of outcomes. The most severe of these would be that the services of the individual would be terminated. Obviously this is a matter of careful judgment on the leader's part, but a number of pastors participating in the church management seminars at Wake Forest University have reported "successful" firings of volunteers. It goes without saying that a written job description that has been reviewed with the volunteer can be of considerable help should the necessity for this extreme action occur.

A continuing effort to review and clarify the expectations that the pastor and people have of one another will result in fewer crises and improved overall management of the church. Still, just because people know what is expected of them and their associates does not necessarily mean that they will, in fact, do what has to be done to have a successful church. It should not come as a surprise, therefore, that the next chapter is concerned with meeting that challenge.

Chapter 8

How to Motivate People

Most church leaders have quite limited resources available for all the things that they need to get done. For this reason they must develop a clear understanding of the nature of influence and learn how to translate that understanding into appropriate actions performed by paid and volunteer personnel of their churches.

In order to identify the mechanism through which a pastor or anyone else influences people, one should possess a basic understanding of human motivation, sources of authority and power, and an appreciation of the dynamics of interaction between individuals and organizations. This chapter addresses these challenges by examining behavioral theories and demonstrating their applications for successful church management.

Motivational Theories

While there are numerous theories which attempt to explain why a person is motivated to act or react in a certain manner, four theories of motivation have been selected as particularly important for our discussions.

Maslow's Hierarchy of Needs

Abraham Maslow's theory of motivation recognizes a hierarchy of human needs. At the base of this hierarchy are physiological needs—air, water, food, and other life supportive resources. Above these, in ascending order, are needs to feel safe and secure, needs for social interaction and love, the need for esteem—to feel that one has value as a human being—and finally, at the top of the hierarchy, the need for "self-actualization." This last term refers to the need to grow toward the realization of one's full potential, whatever that might include.

In considering the implications of Maslow's conceptualization of human needs, it is important to bear several things in mind. First, human behavior is not random—people are seen as moving consciously or unconsciously toward meeting their needs. There is a definite causality involved if others can but trace and comprehend it.

Second, once a need is met, it is no longer a motivator of one's behavior—in Maslow's scheme, the individual becomes "motivated" by higher level needs as the ones below are met to some minimum, "satisficing" degree (the reaching of the minimum level of attainment acceptable in relation to the pursuit of some end or goal as opposed to its full or maximum satisfaction). This degree will vary with individuals for reasons that may be complex, and one should not be misled by the simplicity of Maslow's model to believe that human motivation is uniform or pretty much cut-and-dried once one understands the model.

Third, there is a growth dynamic within every individual, though this force can be stunted or diminished as a result of negative experiences over time. Such experiences are generally advanced as the explanation why some employees seem "beyond recall" motivationally, no matter what approach a supervisor might take with them.

The Three Basic Needs Identified by McClelland

David McClelland's theories of human needs and motivation[1] complement Maslow's theories. McClelland identifies needs for achievement, affiliation, and power as central to understanding one's response to one's environment. Significantly, achievement is viewed as a learned need instead of an innate one. The intensity of this need may vary with different cultures and the societies within that culture. American middle-class society is highly motivated by achievement. Any doubts concerning the validity of this statement may easily be dispelled by asking middle-class parents about their children. Invariably the answer is a checklist of the children's

[1]David McClelland, *The Achieving Society* (New York: The Free Press, 1961), chapter 2.

achievements—both past and present.

While McClelland's need for affiliation closely parallels Maslow's social/love need, he introduces a basic need omitted by Maslow: power. Power needs include the motive for ascendence over others, but more importantly they relate to having a significant degree of control over one's own "life space." In this context one may derive equal satisfaction from rejecting a promotion that could cause a "role overload" as from accepting the more prestigious position.

White's Competence Theory

Robert White's competence theory builds on the theories of Maslow and McClelland. White identifies a strong need to both gain skills and demonstrate these skills to others. By gaining new skills, a person gains increased control over his or her environment, thereby contributing to one's sense of self-esteem.[2]

Reinforcement Theory

B. F. Skinner and other advocates of reinforcement theory offer another approach to understanding human behavior. Reinforcement theory does not attempt to explain why we react to our environment but instead focuses on how we learn to react to that environment. In simple terms, reinforcement theorists suggest that behavior which is associated with pleasure will be continued and experiences that do not promote a pleasurable state will be discontinued. Skinner stresses the de-emphasization of punishment to arrest undesired behavior, feeling that the resentment it often instills may be more detrimental than helpful in teaching desired reactions. Undesirable behavior may be reduced merely by not rewarding it. This presumes, however, that one is able to divine what an individual finds to be rewarding—a question that is sometimes curiously complex.

Applications of Theories of Motivation

Theories provide a basis for thinking about phenomena in an organized way. Thus theory does not necessarily have to be *valid* to be of *value*. Many useful products and processes have been developed out of the application of theories that have subsequently been modified or disproved altogether. While no responsible

---

[2]Robert White, "Motivation Reconsidered: The Concept of Competence," *Psychological Review* (1959), pp. 297-333.

behavioral scientist would hold that the theories of motivation that now exist will never be superceded, these theories do provide managers with a means of conceptualizing the beginning points of human behavior both within and outside of organizational life.

If, for example, the pastor's secretary shows considerable resistance to the addition of a second secretary to the church staff, the pastor might invoke one or more of the theories presented above to gain an insight as to what might be troubling her. This does not mean that the explanation would be readily apparent as a result of doing this, nor does it mean that the pastor ought to substitute speculation guided by theory for talking with his secretary about his perceptions of her discomfort. It does mean that he might approach such an addition to the staff with increased sensitivity as to the possible impact of this change on his secretary. Instead of seeing the addition of another secretary as an act of thoughtfulness on the pastor's part (intended reward), the church secretary might perceive the move as an unverbalized criticism of her ability to handle her work load (White—competence need). If this were her perception, her sense of esteem (Maslow—esteem level) might be diminished to some degree, reducing her sense of security (Maslow—security level) in respect to her job. If the working relationship (Maslow—social/love level) between the pastor and his secretary had been a good one, she might also fear that the addition of another person to the staff would alter that relationship. Related to this might be a sense of loss of control (McClelland—need for power) over conditions related to her work environment.

Again it should be recognized that such interpretation amounts to hypothesizing. Nevertheless, engaging in it can provide insights, increased understanding, and even some ability to predict possible reactions to changes within the staff or other aspects of the church which the pastor might have in mind.

Theories of motivation can also be useful in the formulation of strategies and tactics for managing relationships with volunteers and others whose efforts or agreement are important to the success of the church. This is not to say that the relationships with such persons should be planned every step of the way and devoid of spontaneity, but the relationships are apt to be much better all the way around if the church leader makes an effort to identify and respond to the needs of individuals along with those of the church and himself or herself. At what level or levels of motivation does a person appear to be operating? Is he or she motivated by a desire for the approval and affection of others? What would he or she find most rewarding, public recognition of his or her contributions or being named head of an important committee? In considering what might have significant meaning, bear in mind that whatever meets a human need is, in effect, a reward. This realization is important, of course, in the application of reinforcement theory and is basic to exchange theory, which will be discussed toward the end of the chapter.

Authority and Power

Many people have ambivalent feelings about authority and power. Few people like working under a tyrant, and the strong egalitarian value of our society often leads to a sense of guilt when one is called upon to tell others what to do. Whatever one's feelings about authority and power, the church leader will have to influence others if he or she is to manage the church well; so one ought not to insist on being naive in respect to these phenomena.

Leaders who acquire a sophisticated knowledge of authority and power will realize that they have far more means at their disposal to influence those who assist them with the work of the church than they ever realized. This is likely to be particularly true in respect to those services which are volunteered by influential persons within the community who are not members of the congregation.

Such awareness may also prevent the leaders from using their authority and power at a time when its exercise would be redundant, thereby incurring unnecessary resentment.

Theoretical Bases of Authority and Power

Discussions of authority and power usually point out that these forms of influence are based on the position which one holds, one's person and behavior over time, or preferably both. These same discussions are less instructive as to the practical implications of some of the distinctions that exist between authority and power.

Authority may be defined as the *right* to initiate for other persons, power as the *capacity* to do so. Authority is always legitimated in some manner, as by law, custom, or the willing, voluntary compliance of those whose behavior is being influenced. Power may or may not be legitimated, but the person being directed is inevitably aware that the person who has this form of influence can hurt one if one should not comply with the demands that are being made. These distinctions can be illustrated with some specific examples.

In the military services the ensign or second lieutenant has the authority of position which permits him or her to issue orders to persons with lower rank. However, it is a common experience for the newly commissioned officer to learn that it takes more than rank to get a cagey bunch of experienced enlisted personnel to do what one wants or needs to have them do. Beyond having the rank, the new officer must win the willing compliance of those under him or her by force of his or her personality and actions. Although some will give him or her the benefit of the doubt for a short time, inevitably the vested right that he or she has to influence their actions must be supported by at least some degree of earned respect for him or her in the role of a junior officer if he or she is to be at all effective.

Ultimately the power that any officer has resides in the "Uniform Code of Military Justice," a body of law which directs that a member of the armed forces must follow the order of a superior in rank and prescribes the maximum penalties for not doing so. However, many new officers will be fuzzy as to what constitutes a "legal order," and most will recognize that frequent recourse to the code will hardly impress superiors when they write "fitness reports" for those reporting to them. In this sense power is quite a lot like money. Leaders may have recourse to it but may well find themselves judged, to some degree, in relation to how they spend it.

At the same time, authority and power are not mutually exclusive. It helps to have one's authority buttressed by power. The point to be made here is that the pastor, or other person who has managerial responsibilities, will generally get the best results over time from those whom he or she manages if he or she recognizes the value of voluntary compliance (authority) as opposed to forced compliance (power) and resorts to his or her ability to force particular actions only on rare occasions—when he or she really needs to bring the people into line immediately and on no uncertain terms.

People Accept the Pastor's Authority for a Variety of Reasons

Some church members may comply with initiatives by the pastor because of his or her role of guiding them in understanding religious precepts. Others may simply accept the pastor's influence and accede to it as a matter of tradition. They have been socialized to believe that cooperating with the leadership of an ordained minister is only fit and proper, so long as his or her initiatives are consistent with their understanding of his or her role.

Ordination, of course, is itself a basis of authority. Ordination conveys that the pastor is certified to lead parishioners by virtue of his or her faith, knowledge, and skill. (Societally, in effect, the pastor's authority has developed through tradition to the point where he or she is licensed by our society to lead in religious matters and the related business affairs of the church.)

The Positive Side of Power

Power also exists in one's ability to reward others and/or in their perception that one can do so. Despite the difficulties of conceptualizing the phenomenon called "leadership," those who have studied it are pretty much in agreement that the basic reason why people follow leaders is that people perceive—either consciously or unconsciously—that by doing so they will satisfy their own needs. In other words, those who follow a leader perceive either that acts related to following will be intrinsically rewarding or that following will result in some eventual personal payoff. Thus pastors and other church leaders would do well not only to recognize their sources of authority but also to consider the range of ways in which they can reward those whom they may need or wish to influence.

Moving from theory to its applications in contending with the daily realities of accomplishing God's work on earth, how does one get the sexton to change mop water more frequently, or move the chairman of the church school committee to call a long-overdue meeting and resolve that petty but troublesome issue regarding who gets to use the church basement on Wednesday nights? Reminded of mundane challenges such as these, one must recognize that the pastor, like managers in all areas of human endeavor, needs all of the authority that he or she can muster if he or she is to meet such diverse responsibilities. If the pastor will invest the same degree of imagination that he or she puts into the preparation of a good sermon into the determination of what those who must perform the work of the church are likely to find rewarding, he or she will find that he or she can significantly increase the degree to which these people comply with attempts to initiate for them. By referring to the motivational theories of Maslow, McClelland, and White, the pastor should be able to generate an extensive list of ways to reward these people.

For example, many of us seem to have an insatiable need for affirmation by others. Even those whose self-esteem is reasonably strong and enduring are not exempt from this need. Hence a note, a word of thanks, or a moment of recognition in the presence of others can each bear dividends in the form of a continuing willingness to contribute to the welfare of the church far beyond the time or thought invested in such actions. Clipping an article related to an interest of a committee head and transmitting it to him or her at an appropriate time can make that person feel just a bit special and appreciative. More expensive but possibly an excellent investment for the church, the pastor might identify a seminar or other training opportunity for a member of the staff and arrange for that individual to experience it. Such an opportunity can have lasting returns in the forms of increased competence, personal growth, and recognition.

The important thing for the pastor in this area of responsibility is to get into the habit of identifying potential rewards, large and small, and learning to dispense them wherever and whenever they will promote the work of the church.

More on Translating Theories into Action

All of this is intended to illustrate that, by developing a fuller understanding of the bases from which they can derive authority and power, pastors should find themselves more able to conceive of ways to influence those around them. This should be as true for volunteers as it is for members of the paid staff. It should also be true in respect to members of the vestry or church board, community officials, and local corporate leaders. Obviously, however, there are limits to any individual's authority and power in respect to influencing others, and the development of some sensitivity as to what these limits are for each person whom it is necessary to influence is important. Pastors can then recognize these limits and abide by them, or work toward expanding the scope of actions in respect to which another person will be inclined to comply with their initiatives.[3]

A specific example of this might be the situation in which the pastor sees the need for a new sanctuary but anticipates resistance to tearing down the old one and rebuilding it. Older members of the congregation, in particular, would be likely to resist the change on sentimental grounds if on no other ones.

Such an issue would call for a thorough assessment by the pastor of the sources of the resistance and the likelihood of being able to wield sufficient influence to overcome it. The pastor would need to consider the personalities involved, whether she could influence them to go along with the change—if not to support it actively—and how this might be done. Even if the result of such an assessment might be that she could not overcome the resistance at the time in question, it could result in the formulation of strategy and tactics likely to achieve the desired outcome at a later date. She might, for example, suggest that any new sanctuary incorporate paneling or other features from the existing one or be dedicated to persons with whom the older members would be inclined to identify.

The Development of Exchange Relationships

People often respond to the initiatives of one another out of a sense of obligation rather than because they really like what the other person is proposing. Experienced politicians utilize their knowledge of this phenomenon daily in their relationships with colleagues and constituents, exchanging services of one kind or another for compliance as votes or services controlled by others may be needed. In relation to this mode of interaction, a challenge confronting virtually every pastor is that the church is one of those organizations whose success relies largely on the work of volunteers. Many pastors seem to regard this condition as a tremendous handicap, feeling that the absence of controls over volunteers inherent to an employer-employee relationship makes the work contributions from them unpredictable at best. In other words, these pastors display an anxiety and lack of knowledge about managing interactions in organizational life that are not set forth as formalized authority-responsibility and communications relationships. Such informal patterns, which experts in organizational

[3]The classic discussion of such limits appears in Chester Bernard, *Functions of the Executive* (Cambridge, Mass.: Harvard University Press, 1978), chapter 12.

behavior recognize as crucial to the effective functioning of organizations, are generally referred to as lateral and diagonal relationships. Managers in advisory roles often become quite good at managing such relationships, exerting influence within their organizations far in excess of that which an organization chart would suggest that they could bring to bear.[4]

Exchange Theory

The final theoretical framework that is presented here provides some surprising insights as to how one can influence the behavior of persons in respect to whom one has little or no formal authority. Hence it should be of particular value in relation to the management of volunteers.

As each individual lives his or her life, he or she is dependent to some degree on others for the meeting of his or her needs. One goes to a medical doctor when one is seriously ill, to an auto mechanic when one's car threatens to stop running, and so forth. More intimately, the male depends upon another human being of the opposite sex to enable him to have children and to bear the major responsibilities of raising them. There are literally thousands of examples that one might use to illustrate the ways in which human beings are dependent on one another. We are, significantly, *interdependent.*

Recognizing this, it is revealing to consider the relationship between two people as a series of exchanges between them and to note that the possibilities as to what may be exchanged are virtually endless. Money, physical objects, time, knowledge, skills, and feelings are only a few examples of the multiplicity of things that may be exchanged by two parties in a vast variety of ways.

Norm of Reciprocity Is Universal

Furthermore, as Mauss has noted,[5] there is in virtually all societies a sense of obligation to reciprocate with a factor of approximately equal value anything that the individual has received from another party. For instance, if one person accepts the invitation of another person to dinner at a fine restaurant and enjoys

---

[4]George Strauss, "Tactics of Lateral Relationship: The Purchasing Agent," *Administrative Science Quarterly,* vol. 7, no. 2 (September, 1962).

[5]Marcel Mauss, *The Gift* (New York: W. W. Norton & Company, Inc., 1967), pp. 1-5.

a sumptuous meal and pleasant evening, one then feels—and the host anticipates that one will feel—an obligation to respond with some experience or factor of approximately equal value in the not-too-distant future. If one fails to reciprocate, this will be understood by the host and others who know both of them, as bad manners, a sign that the guest did not wish to have any sort of ongoing relationship with the host, or both.

Though it may seem unattractive as a characteristic of human behavior, most people are very conscious within their network of human relationships as to who "owes" them and to whom they themselves are obligated or "owing." They also make decisions, from time to time, as to which of these "accounts" they wish to close out, either by failing to reciprocate (generally seen as very rude) or by reciprocating but refraining from accepting factors of value from the other party in the future. In this same sense, new "accounts" or relationships are also established and reflect the ongoing exchange of factors of varying value.

Peter Blau, one of the social theorists writing about exchange theory,[6] as this sort of social scorekeeping is termed, has pointed out some of its especially subtle dynamics. In the life of a relationship between two individuals who are presumed to be more or less equal, the inability of one to provide factors to the other of values that either person will be likely to regard as roughly equal often results in one's acceding to the initiatives of the other. In other words, the former subordinates himself or herself to the latter to redress the inbalance of the exchanges between them. However, this assumes that the individual who sees himself or herself as having less to offer than he or she generally receives wishes to continue the relationship. The individual may break away from the relationship instead, feeling diminished by his or her inability to reciprocate in an even, ongoing exchange with the other person.

While the pastor may not wish to take advantage of this behavioral phenomenon in a Machiavellian sense, the awareness of it may enable him or her to gain an insight as to why some of those persons with whom he or she interacts go along with what he or she recommends even when they are not in accord with his or her thinking. At the same time the pastor should understand that many individuals feel no sense of diminishment in subordinating

---

[6]Peter M. Blau, *Exchange and Power in Social Life* (New York: John Wiley & Sons, Inc., 1964), pp. 118–125.

themselves to the leadership of other persons, particularly when they believe that the ends toward which the other person in the relationship is moving are consistent with their own values. In fact this type of voluntary subordination by individuals to the influence of others occurs in informal groups as a matter of course.

William F. Whyte has formulated the principles of exchange theory into a typology of transactions which delineate the various types of exchanges that may take place between two parties[7] He points out that whether the factors which people exchange are felt to have value is a function of the perception, principally, of the receiver. Thus factors offered with the best of intentions may be viewed by the receiver as insulting or punitive, leading the receiver to reciprocate negatively in kind. All of this is to say that there are obviously negative exchanges as well as positive ones, and in a human relationship the understanding by one individual that another is injuring him or her in some way will only lead that person to retaliate, move to interact with the other less frequently, or break off the relationship altogether.

Obviously if the pastor wishes to establish the sort of relationship with another individual that will enable him or her to influence that person's behavior when he or she needs to, the pastor must work at knowing the person well enough to recognize what that person's needs are and create or take advantage of opportunities that he or she has to meet some of those needs. In effect, the pastor will then be perceived by the individual as having contributed in some way to his or her well-being, thereby creating within a sense of obligation to the pastor. Whether the person feels subordinate to the pastor or not in their relationship, he or she will feel a sense of obligation to the pastor and will recognize, in all probability, that one way of squaring this obligation is to go along with the pastor's explicit or apparent wishes.

Balancing Who Initiates for Whom

It is important, however, that the pastor not always be the one in the relationship who does the initiating. Most people become resistant over time to being always the one who is initiated upon. Therefore the pastor needs to ensure that the other person has opportunities to initiate for him or her from time to time. In other

---

[7]William F. Whyte, "Transactions," *Organizational Behavior: Theory and Applications* (Homewood, Ill.: Richard D. Irwin, Inc., 1969), pp. 147-170.

words, there should be a rough balancing of who is placed in the position of responding to the other over the life of the relationship if it is to be a positive one.

William F. Whyte has suggested several principles for influencing another person when one's relationship with the other is essentially an advisory one. An adaptation of this guide is presented below, not only for its value in such relationships but also because it is suggestive of the kind of purposeful approach that one might develop for any sort of lateral relationship.

A Guide for Managing Advisory Relationships[8]

1. First, build a relationship with the person to be advised through reasonably frequent and regular positive interactions.

2. Hold your advice until you sense that you have established a positive personal relationship with the person to be advised. By doing so, you increase the chances that your advice will be accepted.

3. Familiarize yourself with the other person's situation and problems through observation, interviewing, or casual conversation. Create opportunities for the party to explain the situation and problem from his or her own point of view, with an eye toward leading him or her to ask for your thinking about it.

4. Work toward incorporating your advice into an ongoing pattern of positive exchanges between the other person and yourself. Search for things of value that the other person might do for you. The idea is to create a situation in which the other person initiates behavior for you approximately as often as you do for him or her, on balance, over an extended period of time.

5. Try to help the person whom you wish to advise increase the rewards that he or she might receive from persons other than yourself for doing his or her job.

The General Usefulness of Exchange Theory

In addition to the applications of exchange theory that have been suggested in the context of explaining it, the framework is useful in conceptualizing the status and dynamics of the relationship between

---

[8]The above represents a paraphrasing of principles enumerated in *ibid.*, p. 409.

two parties at any level of analysis. For example, if the pastor senses that a member of the congregation is drifting away from the church, the pastor might very well gain some insights as to why by asking himself or herself what perceptions the person may have of what value he or she derives from being an active member of the congregation.

In the same vein the pastor or other church leader must recognize that those who volunteer to perform services for the church rarely do so out of altruism. Although this position may seem cynical and thus offensive, motivation and exchange theories are quite consistent in recognizing that a person meets his or her own needs, first and foremost, through meeting the needs of others. This appears to be an enduring means of enabling one to feel that one is of some consequence.

By volunteering one's services to the church or any other organization, the individual gains recognition and acceptance leading to enhancing self-esteem, along with opportunities to associate with persons of similar interests. Building from this insight, the pastor can work toward the establishment of exchange relationships with individual volunteers in which he or she leads them to believe, quite accurately, that they satisfy their side of the tacit "exchange balance" by meeting the obligations to which they have committed themselves.

The following points, attributed to J. Donald Philips, president of Michigan's Hillsdale College, provide a practical framework for meeting needs that are common to volunteer workers. As such they represent a useful guide to developing positive exchange relationships.

Volunteer Viewpoint[9]

If you want my loyalty, interests and best efforts, remember that . . .

1. I need a *sense of belonging,* a feeling that I am honestly needed for my total self, not just for my hands, nor because I take orders well.

2. I need to have a sense of sharing in planning our objectives. My need will be satisfied only when I feel that *my* ideas have had a fair hearing.

[9]Harriet Naylor, *Volunteers Today: Finding, Training, and Working with Them* (New York: Dryden Associates, 1967, 1973), pp. 18–19.

3. I need to feel that the goals and objectives arrived at are *within reach* and that they make sense to *me*.

4. I need to feel that what I'm doing has *real purpose* or contributes to human welfare—that its value extends even beyond my personal gain, or hours.

5. I need to share in *making the rules* which, together, we shall live and work toward our goals.

6. I need to know in some clear detail just what is expected of me—not only my detailed task but where I have opportunity to make personal and final decisions.

7. I need to have some *responsibilities that challenge,* that are within range of my abilities and interest, and that contribute toward reaching my assigned goal, and that cover all goals.

8. I need to *see* that *progress* is being made toward the goals we have set.

9. I need to be kept informed. What I'm not *up* on, I may be *down* on. (Keeping me informed is one way to give me status as an individual.)

10. I need to have confidence in my superiors—confidence based upon assurance of consistent fair treatment, or recognition when it is due, and trust that loyalty will bring increased security.

In brief, it really doesn't matter how much sense *my part* in this organization makes to *you*—I must feel that the whole deal makes sense to me!

If one were to conclude that exchange theory is as applicable to the pastor's relationship with members of the paid staff as it is to his or her ability to influence those who are volunteers, one would be quite right. The purpose of focusing its application on the managerial challenge presented by volunteers has been to emphasize to the pastor that he or she does in fact have a means of developing some leverage in respect to the problems of influencing these people. Again, some volunteers will respond as readily to the initiatives of the pastor as do the paid members of the staff out of respect for the pastor's position, expertise, or other bases of authority. In the final analysis, whether any individual allows himself or herself to be influenced by another human being is often a complex matter involving motivations that operate at both conscious and unconscious levels. Recognizing this, the pastor can never be confident that he or she has exact knowledge as to why he or she has succeeded or failed in his or her attempts to influence another human being. Usually, however, precise knowledge as to why one has been able to influence another person will count for less than having been able to do so. In this connection it does seem likely that the pastor has more ways of being influential than he or she has previously realized.

Chapter 9

The Administrative Audit

Change is a gradual process in many churches. Turnover in leadership, growth or decline of membership, and shifts in organization and policies tend to be evolutionary changes.

The gradual nature of change and its cumulative impacts in a church are the prime reasons for conducting an administrative audit to identify needs for improvement. In this chapter let's look at what an administrative audit is, what it can do to help, and how it should be carried out.

What Is an Administrative Audit?

An administrative audit is a periodic examination of the managerial effectiveness of the church. In specific terms, a typical audit should embrace the following areas:

1. *The objectives of the church.* Are these spelled out? Do they include both long-term and short-term objectives? Do the appropriate committees know of and refer to the objectives? Do the objectives still fit with the curent directions and intentions of the church?

2. *Current policies.* What are the policies of the church—the statements of how things will be done to work toward the church's objectives? Are the policies written down or simply taken for granted? Do the appropriate people have knowledge of the pertinent policies? Do the written policies make sense in the light of what's actually going on, and what should be going on, in the church's programs?

3. *Current programs.* Does each program have its own objectives and timetables? Are program responsibilities clearly spelled out? Is there a reasonable allocation of resources to ensure accomplishment of programs? Are desired results being achieved?

4. Is there a reasonable *linkage between church objectives and current programs?* An experienced consultant will always look for this linkage and frequently find the lack of it to be a basic cause of managerial ineffectiveness. Programs have changed direction; new programs have been established, and resources (people, money) are now being allocated on a basis that simply does not match with the overall objectives of the church. Rather, programs and resources are responsive to the interests and influence of particular individuals. Another problem arises when one program is difficult to accomplish and another easier, and the easier one gets the effort.

5. *Organization relationships—who's responsible for what?* Even a small church can suffer the problem of unclear responsibility and authority. Shifts of volunteer personnel, overloaded paid staff, and changing priorities as crises arise—all these contribute to abnormal pressures on organizational relationships within a church. Since the church *is* people, this factor is of critical importance in the audit.

6. *Work loads.* Having a reasonable work load is of concern to every person on a payroll and to those in a volunteer role as well. Work load analysis gets into the "nitty-gritty" of evaluating how long it ought to take to do things normally and evaluating whether the package of duties assigned to each person reflects a practical and reasonable expectation of output.

7. *Methods of processing data.* Personalized ways of getting the job done aren't always the most efficient. The church secretary's filing system, the treasurer's billing methods, the music director's control of inventories of hymnals and choir robes—these are all examples of areas where simple improvements can make everybody's job easier. Very often the issue is not money but time, or perhaps just eliminating frustration by doings jobs in an orderly, systematic way.

8. *Financial controls.* It is just good sense to check on the procedures for managing revenues and expenditures. Are the funds moving rapidly to the designated accounts? Are we getting the best practical interest rate on funds, short-term and long-term? Is the control of expenditures only by authorized individuals being observed? Is money being spent at a rate during the year which

assures meeting budget limits by year-end?

An administrative audit needs to be planned carefully right from the outset. It's important to delineate clearly those areas which *need* examination and those which can be left out or covered only briefly. The latter might include areas in which administrative action has been recently taken, for example, new manuals written, policy recently redefined. An administrative audit does not have to replow ground that has been recently tilled.

Who Should Do the Audit?

Normally the people who should be directly involved are the pastor and the governing board of the church, possibly through an audit committee set up temporarily to focus on this task. A consultant might be employed, but this is expensive and probably necessary only where the organization is sufficiently large and the administration problems so complex as to warrant the expense. A medium-sized church that audits itself administratively—say, every five years—and takes action to correct problems noted does not need to bring in a consultant.

Method of Conducting Administrative Audit

The first step in the audit, following initial planning of scope, is to explain the purpose, benefits, and methods of the audit to all paid and volunteer staff. Apprehensions need to be allayed; questions should be encouraged and answered frankly. The pastor should stress the need for cooperation in giving information and help. The schedule for the audit should be explained.

The next step is to assemble and review pertinent written materials dealing with administration of the church. These are likely to include budgets, job descriptions, the personnel policy manual, memos outlining administrative policy and procedures, publications documenting the objectives and role of church committees, and the like. How much written material is available will depend on how formalized administrative practices in the organization are. The lack of such documentation may in itself signal possible problem areas.

The next step is interviewing administrative personnel. Because of the relatively small size of church organizations, the rule of thumb would be to interview all administrative personnel, including both paid staff and key committee people. Normally starting interviews at the top of the organization makes sense in order to develop a consistent and informed "overview" of the administrative process. While the pastor and the chairpersons of the governing board may not know the details, they do see administration as a series of processes designed to fulfill certain objectives of the organization. It is important to develop that perspective at the outset. It may well be that subsequent interviews "down the line" will change those perceptions. But comparison of what *is* taking place administratively against what is *supposed to be* taking place can highlight causes of administrative inefficiencies.

How long should the interviews take? Properly planned, an interview with a "management" person is likely to require one to two hours. Interviews with people who perform clerical, mainte-nance, and other routine functions will take less time.

"Properly planned" is the key to effective use of interview time. For each person interviewed the interviewer should be prepared with key questions pertaining to that position. This technique is important in ensuring that interviews cover the topics that need to be covered, cover them in the appropriate depth, and that needed information is, in fact, gathered.

Interviews should take place at some reasonably quiet location, preferably away from the interviewee's telephone or other interruptions. At the beginning of the interview the interviewee should be put at ease by reminding him or her of the purposes and benefits of the administrative audit. While an administrative audit is focused on procedures, policies, and processes, the factors of personality and emotions inevitably come into the picture. After all, those conducting the administrative audit are specifically looking for problem areas. Those being interviewed will sometimes seize on the interview as an opportunity to vent their feelings about individuals. This situation needs to be dealt with sympathetically but firmly, making it clear that the audit is not a "witch hunt" and that personal frictions will be noted but are not the main issue. One needs to be careful to keep the discussion as objective as possible.

With respect to confidentiality of discussion, assurance can and should be given by the interviewer at the outset. It is important that the interviewer in possession of confidential data of any sort not disclose its source in talking with others. Furthermore, the final report of the administration audit does not identify any single source of comments on problems.

Following each interview the interviewer should follow the practice of writing up notes. Depending on memory simply won't do the job. The interview notes are the raw material from which the findings of the administrative audit are to be drawn.

As the interview process continues, there is often a need to modify interview guides either to probe certain problems that seem to be emerging or to seek out particular hard-to-get data. In some instances call-back interviews will be necessary to supplement or verify information gathered in interviews subsequent to the initial one. However, carefully planned interviews will keep this practice to a minimum.

Up to this point we have talked about two sources of administrative audit information: (1) published manuals, policy and procedure statements, etc., and (2) interviews with people involved in the administrative process of the church.

A third possible source of input to the administrative audit is an agency within the denominational organization that deals with church administration. Of course, where policy and procedure guidelines have been provided by such an agency to your church, these would normally be picked up in reviewing published policies. However, it may also be desirable for the administrative audit person to contact the denominational agency to see about practices followed by other churches, experience with particular problems, services that might be available, and the like. All too often small churches, particularly, do not realize the wealth of useful services and information on administrative processes that may be available through the denomination.

Analyzing the Data

Now the next key stage of the administrative audit is at hand—that of analyzing the data. Here are some tips from a management consultant:

1. First review all the notes from the published data—from interviews and other sources—and establish some broad categories by which to classify the findings. These headings might include: staffing, compensation, financial controls, organization, objectives, facilities, maintenance—just to mention some basic categories.

2. Organize all the collected data according to these categories.

3. Identify and describe the problems that emerge from analysis
    of the data thus classified.

Problem identification is the key to an effective administrative
audit. It has been truly said that "a problem identified clearly is a
problem half-solved."

It is undeniably true that people involved in the administrative
process, whether leadership or workers, tend to intermingle and
confuse symptoms of problems, causes of problems, and the
problems themselves. This is one of the reasons for having
administrative audits done by a person or persons not directly
involved administratively. The "fresh look" is often most valuable
in the problem-definition stage.

The important issue to stress is the need for reviewing the data
carefully and objectively and thoughtfully asking these questions:
"What are the key problems here? Which are symptoms or
evidences of problems? What are the real problems and their
causes?" If there is an administrative audit committee, this is the
point at which committee judgments very often can be useful in
analysis of the data. Such judgment applied at this stage provides a
better basis for eventual recommendations.

Recommendations

And now recommendations are in order. The administrative
audit is not completed until specific, clear, and corrective
recommendations are developed. Here are some guidelines for
dealing with these:

1. Do the recommendations, in fact, address themselves to the
    problems as defined?

2. Will the recommendations, if implemented, solve the
    problem effectively?

3. Are the recommendations practical and realistic? Can they
    be put into effect with present resources, using present
    people, without unreasonable disruption of the organiza-
    tion?

4. What are the other impacts of recommendations in terms of
    changes in policies, procedures, authorities and responsibili-
    ties, organization? Can we live with these?

Reporting

The final result of the administrative audit is the written report. After all, it is necessary to communicate findings and recommendations to members of the church staff and to the appropriate members of the congregation. In fact, some kind of summary report may be desirable for the entire congregation to give them a sense of participation in what is taking place.

The final report need not be a lengthy document. It may be sufficient simply to set forth in writing the following:

1. The purposes and method of the administrative audit with brief detail on the information-gathering process.

2. A summary of key problems.

3. A description of the recommendations agreed upon and the plan for their implementation.

The report identifies what can be done in the short term and what needs to take place over the long term. The report should document schedules for follow-up actions. It should also specify who will be responsible for taking these actions. The report of the administrative audit is in itself a plan of action.

Implementation

Implementation of recommendations normally involves such tasks as these:

1. Rewriting job descriptions to reflect changes in authority, responsibilities, and procedures.

2. Preparing, or redrafting, manuals of policy and procedure in appropriate areas. Or if a manual isn't needed, memorandums from the leadership to the appropriate persons on the staff can be written.

3. Developing or redesigning forms for processing and recording data.

The job of implementing approved recommendations from the administrative audit would normally be done by the pastor, by the pertinent committees whose programs are affected by the recommendations, and/or by appropriate staff personnel of the church. In other words, these recommendations are acted upon by the regular administrative mechanism within the church, not by some special committee.

Longer-term actions are worked into the long-term plan of the church to ensure that they are incorporated in a schedule of implementation and followed up to see that they do take place. These are the logical steps for "tucking in the loose ends" of the administrative audit process.

One points needs reemphasis at this stage. The whole process of improving administrative effectiveness can bog down unless the people who need to change are willing to change. This attitude needs to be developed right from the start. The initial explanation of the purposes and benefit of the administrative audit starts this process. The manner in which interviews are conducted, opinions are sought, confidential information is handled, and problems are verified can all contribute to a cooperative attitude on the part of administrative personnel.

The final step in the administrative audit process is to disband the committee. This may seem so obvious as not to warrant comment. But in accordance with the general tenet of sound administration that organizations be kept as lean as possible, any committee which has served its purpose should be dissolved. Doing this officially affords an opportunity for recognition and thanks to its members for their good job.

When should the process be repeated? If one administrative audit turns out to have been a very good thing, is another equally good? In principle the answer is "yes." But an administrative audit is not an easy task. It takes a lot of time. It should not be repeated every two or three years. Problems of an administrative nature warranting an audit don't develop that fast. It probably is a good idea to schedule an administrative audit on the order of every five years in an organization that is on a reasonable path of growth and change.

Chapter 10

Time Management and the Minister: A Unique Problem

How often I have heard, "But I'm different—those nice principles may work for other people, but they won't work for me." Of all the groups I've worked with on time management, ministers may come the closest to having a unique problem. The usual expectation of minister and congregation alike is that they are 100 percent available—twenty-four hours a day, seven days a week. For example:

Robert is the pastor of a large church in the New York area. Among the congregation are a substantial number of people suffering from emotional problems, such as depression, stress, and just plain loneliness.

Robert feels a strong commitment to counsel these people and goes out of his way to provide all the help he can. It is not uncommon for him to receive a "desperate" phone call in the middle of the night.

Robert feels these interruptions to his work schedule and personal life are justified. At the same time he is concerned about the fact that he rarely has time to prepare his sermon until the night before. He feels he is a good preacher, but last-minute preparation is hurting the quality of his sermons. In addition, there are a number of programs in the church which are languishing from inattention. At home his wife complains bitterly about the all-too-frequent intrusions into family life.

Yes, the minister is in a very personal, service-oriented job. He or she must meet the needs of the people. Often these needs are urgent, desperate, and cannot be delayed. Furthermore, the needs are diverse and complex, ranging from the growing-up pains of teenagers, to marital disturbances, to the alcoholism of a lonely senior citizen. To complicate matters, many of these people think of themselves as the minister's boss—after all, they pay part of his or her salary—and so they feel they have a right to claim some of his or her time.

Then there are the rules of thumb which too often serve as management guidelines for the minister:

—"We believe in the open-door policy" (this means you must smile and say hello to every passerby).

—"Hard work gets results" (translated, this means we will evaluate you on *how much* activity, long hours, and overwork, and not on *what* you do or accomplish).

—"If you want it done right, do it yourself" (means you disregard the importance of delegation—you really can get along without adequate or well-trained church staff).

—"The minister is there to help all of God's children" (translated, this means you never say "no"; you should accommodate every request no matter how trivial).

Obviously there are many elements of the minister's job which make good time management habits difficult. But just because it's difficult doesn't reduce the importance or mean it can't be done. If you, the minister, are to be effective in the work of the Lord—in the face of all the problems—it's absolutely essential to develop the "time management habit," to apply some basic management concepts to your daily life.

The Need for Sound Management Principles

Time has frequently been referred to as our most valuable resource. This is because it is the resource that controls the use of all our other resources—our abilities, talents, training, and experience. You, as a minister, have the ability and opportunity to love, lead, teach, console, help. How well you manage your time will determine how effective you are in utilizing your God-given resources.

The resource, time, is different from other resources. We all have equal shares—168 hours per week. A minister, an executive, the president, a homemaker, and a retiree all have exactly the same 168 hours.

Even if you are rich or persuasive, you can't buy or talk others out of their share. If you need extra time this week to counsel with several emotionally disturbed people in your congregation, from where does it come? Cancel the picnic with the family? Cut out a couple hours' sleep by working late or getting up at 5 A.M.? Skip your jogging this afternoon? Or cut your sermon preparation short (again) this week?

Also, unlike capital resources, you can't save up time, waiting for a better opportunity or until you have a plan. If you waste it, it's gone. If you procrastinate, you've lost an opportunity—maybe forever.

Sometimes 168 hours sounds like a lot of time—a whole week! But if we consider all the commitments we have, most of us are left with precious few hours that we actually control (referred to as "discretionary time"). For example, "maintenance activities" usually occupy around ninety hours per week. These are spent in activities, such as eating, sleeping, getting ready for work, cutting grass, paying bills. If you are a minister of modest means, you probably care for your own house and prepare your own tax return. Your maintenance time is high.

In addition, ministers often report fifty-hour work weeks or more. This leaves only twenty-eight hours to do everything else: time with family, community projects, personal growth activities (reading, seminars, and hobbies), time for recreation and leisure, and free time—time to goof off, relax and think about things. Most ministers I know are involved in many activities, including the diverse functions of the church, community projects, active family lives, and personal growth pursuits.

Additionally, ministers as a group are well trained, well read, intelligent, articulate, concerned, involved people. They have a lot to offer; their contribution is vital to society as a whole as well as to many individuals. The allocation of the ministers' resources—including time—is of crucial importance to the minister, his or her family, and the people he or she serves. Most people in this position experience some level of concern and frustration over the management of their time.

The careful allocation of time to a well-articulated set of goals, consistent with their relative priorities and in accordance with a practical action plan, is the underlying management concept for being effective.

Delineation of Goals

Before examining specific tools for effective time management, it is imperative to distinguish between personal and congregational goals and the means for achieving each of these goals. This may be accomplished by answering several basic questions as they relate to your specific situation:

1. Consider the goals that you made either at the beginning of the year or when you joined your present church. List both personal and congregational goals.

2. Rank these goals. Where do your personal goals fit among congregational goals?

3. How many of these goals have thus far been accomplished?

4. Has the church's growth required sacrifices in your or your family's personal growth?

5. Do the initial goals still appear to be realistic and attainable?

6. What key tasks and activities are required to accomplish these goals? Be specific.

7. Rarely are goals effectively accomplished without a commitment to a definite time frame. What deadlines can be set to ensure the accomplishment of the tasks listed in #6?

A Framework for More Effective Time Management

Now let us turn to constructing a practical framework which can facilitate effective time management (TM) planning.

Exhibit 10-1 shows a four-step process to aid the minister in managing his or her time more effectively. This simple problem-solving technique is one frequently employed by managers:

Step 1: Analysis starts out with the collection of information, analysis of the data, and a clear statement of the problems. If meetings consume substantial portions of your time, what kind of meetings? How much time? What are the causes?

Step 2: The *planning* step. What are you trying to accomplish? What is the priority relative to other demands on your time? Do you know what it will take to accomplish it? How long?

Exhibit 10-1

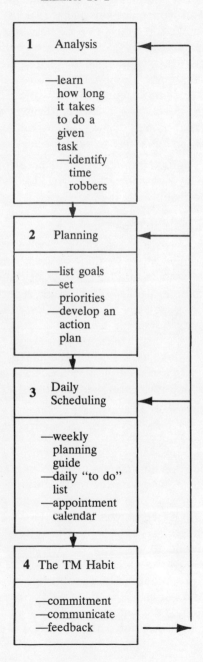

1   Analysis

—learn
how long
it takes
to do a
given
task
—identify
time
robbers

2   Planning

—list goals
—set
priorities
—develop an
action
plan

3   Daily
Scheduling

—weekly
planning
guide
—daily "to do"
list
—appointment
calendar

4   The TM Habit

—commitment
—communicate
—feedback

Step 3: Daily scheduling is the implementation. How do you schedule your time? Do you have a daily "to do" list? How do you make sure you spend the time you need on long-term, important projects, such as the revitalization of the youth program, as well as on the pressing emergencies and frequent interruptions?

Step 4: The *control* step. It means working to develop the *TM habit,* developing a commitment, communicating with others. We must reanalyze our trouble spots, modify our plans, and continue to work to improve.

Now let's follow through each of these four steps with some examples and worksheets so that you, too, can acquire the time management habit.

Step 1—Analysis of Time Use

There are three reasons for analyzing where your time goes. First, our perceptions—where we think we spend our time—are usually grossly inaccurate. Consider the case of the insurance salesman who, after keeping a time log for a week, reported great surprise at finding he was spending in excess of forty minutes a day in and waiting for the elevator in his office building. The statement was hardly out of his mouth when the revelation came, "Hey, I know why that is—I don't have a logical schedule for grouping my outside calls." Yes, he was commiting a cardinal sin of good selling practice.

Ministers find similar revelations. Recall Robert, the person in the incident at the beginning of this chapter. Robert felt the need to control the many interruptions which get in the way of doing other important tasks. Yet these interruptions are a big part of his job, and there are many emergency calls which he had to take. After reading a book on time management, Robert noticed particularly a section on controlling interruptions. The author provided a handy work sheet for analyzing interruptions for a couple of days. Robert decided to try it (see Exhibit 10-2 for the work sheet and a few of Robert's entries).

Robert found to his surprise that, out of the hundred-odd interruptions over a three-day period, there were only two of emergency proportions. All the rest could have been deferred, at least for a short time.

Robert found other interesting things from his log. There were four people who interrupted him several times each day. And there were two matters about which he received phone calls from several different people. A brief note with copies to the interested parties would have been more efficient. He was also surprised at the length of some of the calls and the amount of small talk and socializing.

From his analysis of the log Robert developed several steps for controlling his interruptions.

First, he considered ways to screen all but the emergency calls during a two-hour "quiet period" each day. He could always be reached in an emergency, but except for an emergency he was tied up in important church business at those times.

Second, in the case of people with whom he frequently interacts, he accumulated several items of business and covered them in a less-frequent phone call or meeting.

Thirdly, he organized his phone calls by making several at a time, noting things to be covered, and having all the relevant information available.

The second reason for keeping a time log is to assist in planning. Most of us grossly underestimate the time required to accomplish specific tasks. Are you realistic about how long it will take to prepare for next week's Bible study class or prepare the budget for the proposed crisis control center? Or are you like me—underestimate by 100 percent and wonder why you can't get everything done? A time log gives you accurate data on "how long." It will make your planning more realistic.

The third reason for a time log analysis is that it will allow you to develop some standards or benchmarks against which to measure improvement. If Robert's six hours a day of interruptions are too high, what is reasonable? What is a realistic goal to strive for in thirty days? Six months? Maybe for Robert it's from six hours to five—eventually to four. Robert should keep another interruptions log periodically to measure his progress. Maybe eventually he should strive to get to three hours per day—half of what he's doing now.

Once you have this time log, analyze it for "time robbers." A time robber is an activity which occupies a lot of your time but which doesn't produce a corresponding amount of value. A list of common time robbers for ministers and a time robber analysis work sheet are provided at the end of the chapter (Exhibits 10-4 and 10-5).

If you have not done so recently, I would encourage you to keep a time log for a week. Record the things you do in ten- to

Exhibit 10-2

Robert's Log of Interruptions

Who	Subject	Elapsed Time	Priority	Ideas for Shortening or Eliminating
Mrs. Sheppard	Wanted to know the date of the bazaar—proceeded to discuss last Sunday's sermon in much detail.	18 mins.	C	Should have had Pat (Robert's secretary) take a message because I was working on the budget—Pat could have answered her question.
Jim Conners (Chairman of Finance Committee)	Had some suggestions on how to cut the education budget—most of them can't be done—chatted about last night's basketball game.	24 mins.	B	This call took about 25 minutes—at least twice what it should have taken—cut out some of the socializing.
Pat	Came in with some questions about this week's bulletin.	8 mins.	C	Should have been able to figure it out herself.

Name	Description	Time	Priority	Notes
Jim Conners	Had another idea about the education budget.	11 mins.	B	A new idea every five minutes—probably ought to schedule a luncheon meeting to cover all of these budget matters at one time—started to talk about the game again—cut him off with "got to get back to the figures."
Pat	More questions about the bulletin.	5 mins.	C	Probably should schedule a briefing meeting with her each week to cover all this.
Selma (Robert's wife)	When will I get home—pick up coffee, bread and salad dressing—Robby got in a fight, etc., etc.	15 mins.	C	Another 15 minutes shot—should have had Pat take a message unless it was an emergency.
Anne Reynolds	Paul had a heart attack—meet her at the hospital.		A	There goes the budget!

fifteen-minute intervals. And do it as you go along. Don't wait until the end of the day because you will forget and the record will be inaccurate. Then use the aforementioned work sheets to analyze your time use, your main time robbers, their causes, and their solutions.

Step 2—Planning

Planning makes us *effective* users of time, not just efficient users. To be a good preacher, a good writer, or a good homemaker, you must allocate time for working on the important tasks.

Planning for effective TM requires a current list of goals, the establishment of the relative priorities, and a systematic method for action.

1. *Listing Goals.* It is helpful to list goals in several categories:

a) Job and Career. Ministers often have difficulty thinking about their personal career separately from their job—the church. Certainly there are high-priority goals that you should have for your church. Some of these are short-term, such as increasing the pledges 20 percent this year. Others are longer term, such as financing and constructing a new church school building in five to seven years.

But you should also have goals established for your career. Again, some of these may be short-term, such as increasing your counseling skills by taking two courses at the university this year. Others may be more long-term, such as being the rector at a larger church of about 2,000 communicants in a five- to ten-year period. Start your goal-setting process right now by listing both short- and long-term job and career goals.

b) Family. Most people have a tough time being explicit about family goals. I find it helpful to put family goals in three subdivisions. The first is your family's *life-style.* What's important to your family? A large house? Entertaining? Travel? Vacations? Educational opportunities? Saving for retirement? Talk these things over with other members of the family. Is there general agreement? If not, try to resolve the differences.

A second category is family *financial planning.* It's fine to aspire to travel extensively or to have enough money saved to retire when you're sixty, but can you afford it? Can you put together a financial plan to support it? Usually there's a gap. What's more important? What can you do without? Is education more important than the travel to Mexico? Can you do without the second car? Can your spouse work a few years to make possible the building of a new house?

Make a list of life-style and financial goals, ranking them according to an A, B, C priority system. Discuss these goals with other family members. Make sure the financial plan is consistent with your life-style goals.

The third category of family goals relates to *short-term activities* intended to build communication and strengthen relationships. It may be a shopping trip with a daughter to discuss plans for college, or dinner with your spouse to iron out a disagreement about some bills. Perhaps a picnic one evening with the whole family, who have been too busy going their own way lately to enjoy some fun together.

Many ministers already do this—automatically—because they are sensitive to family interrelationships. But many do not. Are there gaps in your communication with other family members? Is everyone in your family going his or her own way without sharing problems and experience? Do you too often come home tired and flop in front of the TV without concern for the needs and difficulties of others in the family?

c) Community Activities. Most ministers feel an obligation to be active in the community in projects other than those which relate directly to their church. Do you feel you're pulling your load? Or are you into too many projects? Are you doing things that have value and are satisfying to you? Or did you get pushed into too many activities in which you have little interest?

Take an inventory of the community projects in which you are presently engaged. Are they worth doing or aren't they? Are you making a real contribution or not? Are there some you would like to phase out? Others you would like to add? What are realistic goals for your community activities?

d) Personal Goals. The final category of goals are personal or self-goals. Often ministers feel they shouldn't have goals just for themselves. But most do; and if you are honest with yourself, I think you'll find you do, too.

Maybe you'd like to be in better physical shape. If that's your goal, how about joining the special physical fitness program at the "Y"? Maybe you'd like to have a regular tennis game two afternoons a week. Or a little time to read for pleasure. Is there a hobby you enjoy but don't have time to do any more? Consider

Exhibit 10-3

Action Plan for a Youth Program

A-Priority Goal: To develop a more vigorous youth program;
—increase activities
—increase participation in the activities
—reduce the number of youth that drop out of the church when they go to work or off to college

Starting Date: Sept.
Achieve goal by:
2 years from now

KEY PERFORMANCE TASKS/ACTIVITIES (must be done to achieve goal)	RESOURCES NEEDED (money, people, time)	WHEN (Completion date)
1. Draft feasibility study for consideration by the vestry, youth panel, and other key people—survey other churches for input data.		Sept.-Oct. this year
2. Prepare detailed program plan and budget—obtain commitment—expanded budget for next year.	Increase youth program budget $12,500	Nov.-Dec. this year
3. Free up 6 hours/week of my time to work on setting up programs; reduce time on United Way activities.	6 hours/week my time	Starting October this year

Task	Resource	Date
4. Get volunteer to head committee (someone like Sam Burke or Van Gallo).	3-4 hours/week volunteer time	October this year
5. Organize volunteer structure to manage.	4-5 volunteers for activities	November this year
6. Details of activities—get priorities—allocate budget funds.		December this year
7. Start up Phase I activities.		January next year
8. Evaluate Phase I activities.		June next year
9. Prepare, submit, and get approval for Phase II program (Year 2).	Estimated youth budget for Year 2 $18,500	August next year
10. a) Implement Phase II programs. b) Evaluate Phase II.		a) Sept. next year b) the following June

some of your personal goals. It might be helpful to list these goals and designate how and when they can be met.

2. *Priorities.* Having listed your goals, the next step is to set priorities. Try using the ABC system, and fit them into rankings of high value (A-priority), medium value (B-priority), and low value ones you could do without (C-priority).

Next take your A-priority goals and rank them. A-1 is the most important—the one you want to start working on right now. Then decide on second most important, the A-2, and so forth. You can't work on all your goals at once; so it's important to establish which is most important and get to work on that one with whatever time you have available.

3. *The Action Plan.* Making a list of goals and establishing priorities, however, are not enough. A goal is an end to be accomplished—the result of successfully completing a series of tasks. The action plan organizes these tasks according to four procedural steps:

a) List key tasks that must be done to achieve the goal.

b) Arrange the tasks in a logical sequence for working on them.

c) Specify any resources (i.e., time, study, reference materials) which are needed for carrying them out.

d) Develop a timetable for accomplishing the tasks that is consistent with the time and other resources you can allocate to this goal.

The work sheet shown in Exhibit 10-3 illustrates the action plan. It is filled in with entries for a youth program one minister set for a goal. Draw up this work sheet for your own use. Try laying out action plans for your high-priority goals. Start out with an overview of the key tasks and an overall time frame. Some of the details can be filled in later as you go along. Don't worry about possible later changes in the plan—most plans have to be modified from time to time. In fact, you need to review your plan frequently to see how you're progressing and what elements need modifying.

In summary, systematic planning and the allocation of your time accordingly will help you fulfill your mission as an effective minister.

Step 3—Daily Scheduling

Now that you have action plans for accomplishing your high priority goals, the next step is implementation. This means scheduling your time so that you accomplish the key tasks in your plans. The trouble is that ministers have many day-to-day tasks—phone calls, hospital visitations, crises, meetings, drop-in visitors, a mountain of correspondence and paperwork tasks—your daily routine. Much of your daily routine has an element of urgency; it must be done and soon. One of your key volunteers must talk to you. A child was just injured in your day-care center. The bishop is on the phone. The deadline for getting the bulletin to the printers is noon today, and you haven't finished writing it.

On the other hand, the key tasks in your action plans are long-term in nature and can be deferred. "I'll get at that tomorrow." "Let me clear the paperwork off my desk; then I'll be ready to tackle that big job." But tomorrow never comes.

A systematic process of daily planning is essential to achieve a balance between time used for the daily routine and the more important but deferrable tasks in our action plans. One useful tool is the appointment calendar recording meetings, appointments, and perhaps important due dates for tasks (for example, finish the budget).

A second tool for many of us is the "to do" list or "things to do." These lists can be very effective but may also create problems. First, they are not updated every day. We're under a lot of pressure, and we feel we don't have time. Or it's kind of an easy day, and we don't feel the need. Sometimes the phone starts ringing, and we simply forget about it. Thus at the end of the day we haven't done all the tasks we set out to do.

The other problem is that the tasks are not ranked according to their importance. We need to establish a code of priorities and, whenever possible, undertake the tasks in order of their priority. The best use of your time right now is to work on your A-1 priority task. But if you haven't established the priorities in the terms of importance, then you will tend to operate according to a different priority system, such as the first piece of paper in your "in basket"; the short, easy tasks which can be checked off your list quickly; or several less important phone calls that may be more interesting.

"To do" lists, to be really effective, should be updated every day. It should be done early in the morning or late in the day but at a time when you have a few quiet minutes to think and plan. And finally priorities should be set and followed whenever possible.

There's a third type of daily scheduling I would strongly

recommend to ministers: *The Weekly Planning Guide*. The guide allows you to look at current commitments, schedule a key meeting, block out times for A-priority tasks, and schedule plenty of flexible time to handle routine phone calls, correspondence, and other daily activities. A minister's week revolves around Sunday worship service. Probably the best time for you to do this planning is sometime Monday. The planning guide can take a variety of forms and can be adapted to your personal needs. It's as simple as taking a blank piece of paper, drawing up a form, and making photocopies or using an 8½″ x 11″ week-at-a-glance calendar sheet.

The most important aspect of this process is scheduling according to priority. We must schedule A-priority tasks among all the routine paperwork, interruptions, and emergencies. You can do this only by taking time away from the less important tasks—by shortening, deferring, or eliminating some of them.

A final thought concerning priorities. Many people complain that they seem to have too many A priorities—"everything is an A." I like to reserve the A designation for *my* A's—tasks that relate to my important goals. There are, of course, a lot of other tasks that are urgent, perhaps because the chairman of the governing board asks us to, or because a church member has a need. I designate these urgent tasks X. This keeps me from confusing my A priorities with other people's A's.

Step 4—Develop the TM Habit

At the beginning of this chapter we cited some of the problems of being a good manager of time. It's easier *not* to keep a time log. It takes time and effort, and sometimes it is embarrassing to see how much time we really waste. It's tough to plan, set priorities, and stick with them. It's easier to do the short, pleasant task than the tough one we've been dreading and puttting off for a month.

For us to be effective time managers, the process must become part of us—"internalized" is the behavioral term. We must develop good habits to replace the sloppy ones. Unless we keep working at TM, we will regress to the sloppy habits again.

There are three ways that will help you develop the TM habit:

1. *Commitment.* Unless you are committed to improving your time management, forget it. There are no gimmicks or shortcuts. It is apparent that someone lacks commitment when he or she says, "I didn't have time to plan," or "I didn't have time to keep a time log,"

or "I can't control interruptions." Anyone can do these things if he or she wants to. It's your time, and it's within your power to control it as you deem best— if you make up your mind and have the will to do so. But it requires commitment.

2. *Communication.* Ministers are in a service business. They have frequent interaction with many people. They do not operate in a vacuum. Their time management is affected by many other persons. Communicating about time management problems is essential if really good time management habits are to be developed. This means communicating priorities, admitting to limitations and conflicts, learning to say "no" graciously, following up on deadlines, and sharing problems and experiences with other ministers.

3. *Followup and Feedback.* This is the control step, essential to any management process. If you've identified interruptions as your major time problem and decided on some ways to control them, you've come a long way but still aren't through. As any good manager knows, there must be control and feedback. Are you accomplishing what you set out to do? How well? Have you reduced the excess time spent on interruptions one-half hour or one hour? What problems have you encountered in trying to control interruptions? How can you overcome these? What other methods might you try? Perhaps you need to reanalyze—another interruptions log. Or try a different daily scheduling method.

Our world changes; our goals change, and so do our time management problems. Followup and feedback are vital to the time management habit.

Summary

The time management problems of the minister are not easy. The service he or she provides is extremely demanding, the expectations for performance high, and the support he or she gets minimal. Effective management of time is important as well as difficult. We have seen some of the problems and developed a framework for improving. Let's summarize with a few key ideas:

1. The idea of better time management should not be looked on as an overwhelming task of organizing all of your time or using all of it efficiently.

What you need is a chunk of time now and then to do tasks which will lead to achieving important personal goals. Rather than all day

Exhibit 10-4

Frequent Time Robber List

Using this list of frequent time robbers often experienced by ministers, rate your time problems:

	Big Problem for Me	Often a Problem	Seldom a Problem
PLANNING			
1. Not setting goals	___	___	___
2. No daily plan	___	___	___
3. Priorities not clear or changing	___	___	___
4. Leaving tasks unfinished	___	___	___
5. Fire fighting/crisis management	___	___	___
6. No self-imposed deadlines	___	___	___
7. Attempting too much/unrealistic time estimates	___	___	___
ORGANIZING			
8. Personal disorganization/cluttered desk	___	___	___
9. Volunteer groups/committees poorly organized—too much dependency on me	___	___	___
10. Tasks associated with Sunday services not organized	___	___	___

11. Church programs disorganized

DIRECTING

12. Tend to do everything myself
13. Involved in too many routine details
14. Ineffective delegation to staff and volunteers
15. Frequent lack of motivation
16. Not managing conflict well
17. Not coping with change

CONTROLLING

18. Telephone interruptions
19. Drop-in visitors
20. Lack of self-discipline
21. Too many interests
22. No "quiet" time
23. Running out of time for sermon preparation
24. Bogged down with routine details
25. Church business fills in too many of my evenings and days off

Exhibit 10-4—page 2

	Big Problem for Me	Often a Problem	Seldom a Problem
COMMUNICATING			
26. Meetings—too many, too long, not effective enough			
27. Poor communication			
28. Failure to listen to suggestions and concerns			
29. Socializing—drop-in visitors and phone calls			
DECISION MAKING			
30. Snap decisions—not enough consideration of various views of the congregation			
31. Indecision/procrastination			
32. Asking for too many views about everything			
33. Leaving too many decisions up to volunteer committees			
34. Perfectionism			

35. Wanting to please everyone

PERSONAL AND FAMILY

36. Not enough time with my family

37. Poor communication with my spouse

38. Bringing home church problems

39. Church business interrupting family time

40. Not enough time to keep physically fit

41. I'm getting stale—not growing

42. I'm not enjoying my job

43. I don't have time for my hobby

44. Too many community activities—they're a grind

45. Life isn't fun any more

every day, it's an hour or two a day, or a couple of mornings a week, or a long weekend every month or two. Time to do the research for a key sermon, to plan the next all-member canvass, or to spend with your teenage daughter who is having trouble adjusting to a new school.

2. Interruptions and responding to crises are part of your job. Allow plenty of flexible time for the unforeseen. Don't overschedule—you'll only get frustrated.

3. Plan a quiet time in your schedule each day or on most days. Earn this quiet time by shortening, deferring, or eliminating certain less important tasks.

To do this, analyze your time use and find your big problems. Look for causes and workable solutions. Experiment with solutions. Talk to others to get ideas and learn from their experience.

4. Communicate your schedules to your spouse, secretary, and others who are involved in your daily activities. Communicate your problems to your governing board to let them know what's going on and get their help and support. Reinforce what you are doing by talking with others about common problems.

5. Concentrate on effectiveness. Efficiency is defined as doing something right—effectiveness is doing the right something.

6. There's no replacement for planning. A few minutes of planning may save you hours of doing low-value tasks, starting and stopping, shuffling papers, procrastinating.

7. Learn sound principles of delegation, communication, running meetings. They're as important in managing a church as they are in running a business.

8. The causes of most time management problems are internal to ourselves. It has been demonstrated over and over again that internal causes far outweigh external causes such as interruptions. Therefore the power to improve rests primarily within ourselves.

9. It's your life. Whatever you achieve must be done by managing some of your 168 hours. If you refuse to adopt some reasonable time management habits—or rationalize the need away—you jeopardize the opportunity to achieve what you want to in life.

The objective of effective TM is to help you achieve your goals whatever they are—a good job as a minister, a good family life, or a little free time to go down to the lake and fish.

Exhibit 10-5

Time Robber Analysis

A. Describe your #1 time robber _____

_____

_____

B. How bad is it?
How many hours a day do you spend at it?   _____ hrs/day

How many hours should you spend at it?   _____ hrs/day

Estimate your effectiveness in using that time:
_____% effectiveness

Estimate your efficiency in using that time: _____% efficiency

C. List as many causes for the time robber as you can. Be specific! Do you need to do some more analysis to determine better the causes?

D. Now look for solutions to the time robber. List them opposite their appropriate causes creatively! List ones even if they sound "way out." Get a personal friend or co-worker to help you.

E. Set a target for yourself:

—How much would you like to reduce the time spent on the time robber?   _____ hrs/day

—How effective and efficient would you like to become?
_____ % effective _____ % efficient

F. Commitment time! Commit right now to a target you think is realistic to achieve in the next thirty days.

My target: _____

Pick out the two or three solutions which are most likely to achieve that target and work at them:

Solution #1 _____

_____

Solution #2 _____

Solution #3 _____

G. Followup. In thirty days analyze your time robber to see if you've met your target. If not, why not? What got in your way? What additional solutions could you attempt to achieve or better your goal? Again, talk to a friend or a couple of co-workers to see what solutions they might come up with.

APPENDIX

Implications of the Future

One of the fastest-growing bodies of research in management is "futurism," which is also called futurology, exploratory planning, or alternative futures. Corporations, government agencies, and institutions of all sorts are "exploring the future" in order to assess possible opportunities and problems and to devise strategies to deal with them.

What is futurism? How can churches benefit by using futurism as an input to their management decisions?

What Is Futurism?

Futurism is the identification of very long-term (five to twenty-five years) trends; assessment of their direction and rate of change; and evaluation of their impact on society and on the institution conducting the exploration of the future. (The term "institution" is employed to embrace profit and nonprofit organizations as well as sectors of society, such as labor, government, etc.) Analysis of the future is an enormously exciting, intellectual adventure. But its fundamental purpose is to facilitate planning a desired future for the institution in light of likely developments in the environment.

The acceleration of futurism as an arm of managerial thinking appears to stem from several factors. The most important of these is the rate of change, both in technology and society, which makes it imperative, particularly for institutions, to project their future environment to avoid being taken unawares by future developments.

In this context of accelerating societal change the importance of futures analysis to churches becomes apparent. The church as an institution deals with people within their societal framework. As that framework changes, it impacts in varying ways on the church. Forecasting the nature and extent of these impacts is what futurism is all about.

Recognizable Trends of Change

Some of the commonly accepted trends that are already apparent today and will be significant in the future include these:

1. *Urbanization.* Both in the United States and abroad the development of the "megalopolis" is clearly in sight, whether it is the Boston-New York-Washington corridor, in France, or along the islands of Japan. Urbanization as a trend impacts on trends in personal values, qualities of life, social interactions, economics, and energy needs (this is the futurism concept of "cross-impact" of major trends).

2. *Increasing leisure time.* In the reduction in the work week, attitudes of people toward leisure, quality of life, and in increasing affluence to enjoy leisure we again see the cross-impact of trends.

3. *The "knowledge society."* This term is used to describe the effects of increasing levels of education as well as the industrial environment in which modern techniques (i.e., computer-based information systems) require increasing levels of education. A related trend is that of the *information explosion.*

4. *Changing role of the family.* Family structures, family attitudes, family values, physical surroundings of the family, the generation gap, value shifts of upcoming generations—all impact not only on the way in which people live but also on their views toward society, their responsibilities, and their needs for internal values.

5. *Demographic change.* Older people are getting older. We are going through a cycle of changing demographic relationships between young, middle-aged, and older groupings. Incomes are on the rise, but so is inflation. There are major shifts in where people live in the United States, and the structure of communities is in constant flux. Any minister can recite the impact of these changes on the church.

For those interested in exploring these trends further a brief bibliography on futurism is in the Bibliography. The above synopsis has been presented simply to illustrate trends which are only too familiar to ministers because they see their impacts every day on the growth or nongrowth of their church, on the attitudes of their parishioners, and on their perception of the role of religion in society in the next fifteen to twenty-five years.

Ministers are raising questions with great frequency on how the church can deal with these changes. The message here is that futurism is a recognized scholarly discipline for arriving at usable judgments about the future.

How Can Your Church Relate Trends to Its Planning?

Futures analysis, to be useful to your church, needs to be linked to the decision-making process. The linkage is through the church's planning process as discussed in chapter 2, "Strategic Planning."

Since futures analysis deals with the future out beyond the normal long-range planning horizon (i.e., five years or so), the first link is between futures analysis and five-year planning.

A church that does not use the planning process as a way of managing its affairs will have considerable difficulty in relating its judgments on the likely future to today's decisions. In light of this caution, let's look at some specifics as to what a church can do both to assess the future and to relate that assessment to decisions it faces.

First is the problem of gathering information about the future. My first observation would be, "Don't try to reinvent the wheel." There are many books today that provide more than adequate information about basic long-term trends (see the Bibliography). Reference to two or three of these will demonstrate the recurrence in each of the texts of certain basic societal and technological trends. This data base is enough to get started.

The next step might well be an educational effort. Ask a group of thoughtful and concerned church members to make a contribution to the church's planning. I am not suggesting a long-range planning committee per se. It might be desirable to pick only one member of the planning committee and surround that person with four or five others not on the committee. Their charge might be along these lines: "Each of you review this book or that article on future trends; prepare yourself with notes on which of these trends you see impacting on our church and in what ways. Then let's assemble to discuss these impacts."

After doing their homework, the group could then meet to form judgments on:

1. Which are the most significant trends?
2. What is the likelihood of their development, in the opinion of this group, and in what manner will they develop?
3. What impacts might the developing trends have on the church, the congregation, people's attitude toward religion?
4. In the light of these judgments on trend impacts what might that mean in terms of the church's own planning for the future? Specifically how might they affect the church's goals, strategies, program offerings, and allocation of budget resources?

When this task is done, the futures analysis group then meets with the long-range planning committee to pass on results of its work. In this manner the planning process is used as the linkage between the church's decisions and the analysis of the future. The planning committee will find its own ways of relating the futures analysis to the detail of long- and short-term plans.

Conclusion

The roots of our churches go back a long way in time. Changes come slowly. The role of the church in one sense is to resist the changes which buffet it.

This buffeting can produce erosion if the church resists change unreasonably. Conversely, the church can renew its sense of mission and be an increasing source of strength to people bewildered by a changing society. It can be all of these things if the church itself, and your church specifically, is able to anticipate the nature and direction and amount of change that is likely to develop.

Futurism, like other aspects of managerial planning, does not have as its aim an assertion that "this is what the future will be like." Rather, it has as its aim the development of greater awareness and understanding of what the future might be like depending on what assumptions we want to make. If we fail to make any assumptions—because "who knows what the future will bring?"—we will take no action. Inaction is a basic source of instability in institutions.

Bibliography

General Church Administration

Ditzen, Lowell Russell, *The Minister's Desk Book*. Englewood Cliffs, N.J.: Parker Publishing Company, imprint of Prentice-Hall, Inc., 1968.

Graves, Allan W., *Using and Maintaining Church Property*. Englewood Cliffs, N. J.: Prentice-Hall, Inc., 1965.

Gray, Robert N., *Managing the Church, Vol. 1, Church Business Administration*. Enid, Okla.: The Haymaker Press, Inc., 1976.

Gray, Robert N., *Managing the Church, Vol. 2, Business Methods*. Enid, Okla.: The Haymaker Press, Inc., 1976.

Lambert, Norman M., *Managing Church Groups*. Dayton, Ohio: Pflaum Press, 1975.

Lindgren, Alvin J., *Foundations for Purposeful Church Administration*. Nashville: Abingdon Press, 1965.

Lundquist, Helmer C., and Pendorf, James G., *Church Organization: A Manual for Effective Local Church Administration*. Wilton, Conn.: Morehouse-Barlow, Inc., 1977.

Smith, Charles M., *How to Become a Bishop Without Being Religious*. New York: Doubleday & Co., Inc., 1965.

Walz, Edgar, *Church Business Methods: A Handbook for Pastors and Leaders of the Congregation*. St. Louis, Mo.: Concordia Publishing House, 1970.

Decision Making, Leadership, Role of Pastor
(Chapters 1, 7, and 8)

Asch, S., "Studies of Independence and Conformity: A Minority of One Against a Unanimous Majority," *Psychological Monographs,* (1956), pp. 1-70.

Barnard, Chester, *Functions of the Executive.* Cambridge, Mass.: Harvard University Press, 1938.

Blau, Peter M., *Exchange and Power in Social Life.* New York: John Wiley & Sons, Inc., 1964.

Bridston, Keith R., *Church Politics.* New York: World Publishing Co., 1969.

Faust, Clarence H., "The Care and Feeding of Institutions," *Saturday Review* (March 30, 1968), pp. 12-16.

Glasse, James D., *Putting It Together in the Parish.* Nashville: Abingdon Press, 1972.

Harrison, Paul M., *Authority and Power in the Free Church Tradition.* Carbondale, Ill.: Southern Illinois University Press, 1971.

Hiltner, Seward, *Ferment in the Ministry.* Nashville: Abingdon Press, 1969.

Johnson, Douglas, "The Denomination: What's in It for Us?" *Christian Ministry* (May, 1973), pp. 11-13.

Kernohan, Frances K., "Uses of Volunteers in Public Welfare, a Progress Report." *The Observer.* Junior League of the City of New York (January, 1965).

Kotter, John P., *Power in Management.* New York: American Management Association, 1979.

Lee, Robert, *The Social Sources of Church Unity.* Nashville: Abingdon Press, 1960.

Leiffer, Murray H., *The District Superintendent in the United Methodist Church.* Evanston, Ill.: Bureau of Social and Religious Research, 1971.

Maslow, Abraham, *Motivation and Personality.* New York: Harper & Row, Publishers, Inc., 1954.

Mauss, Marcel, *The Gift.* New York: W. W. Norton & Co., Inc., 1967.

McClelland, David C., *The Achieving Society.* New York: The Free Press, 1961.

Metz, Donald L., *New Congregations: Security and Mission in Conflict.* Philadelphia: The Westminster Press, 1967.

Niebuhr, H. Richard, *The Social Sources of Denominationalism.* Magnolia, Mass.: Peter Smith, 1963.

Rusbuldt, Richard E.; Gladden, Richard K.; Green, Norman M., Jr., *Local Church Planning Manual.* Valley Forge: Judson Press, 1977.

Schaller, Lyle E., *The Decision Makers: How to Improve the Quality of Decision Making in Churches.* Nashville: Abingdon Press, 1974.

Schaller, Lyle E., *The Change Agent.* Nashville: Abingdon Press, 1972.

Schaller, Lyle E., "Will the Third Great Awakening Miss the Churches?", *Together* (May, 1973), pp. 15-16.

Shoemaker, Denis E., "Ecclesiastical Future Shock: The Ordeal of Restructuring," *Christian Century* (March 14, 1973), pp. 312-15.

Skinner, B. F., *Walden Two.* London: MacMillan & Co., 1959.

Strauss, George, "Tactics of Lateral Relationship: The Purchasing Agent," *Administrative Science Quarterly,* vol. 7, no. 2 (September, 1962), pp. 161-186.

Weber, Max, "The Three Types of Legitimate Rule," in Etzioni, Amitari, ed., *Complex Organizations.* New York: Holt, Rinehart & Winston, 1961.

White, Robert, "Motivation Reconsidered: The Concept of Competence," *Psychological Review* (1959), pp. 297-333.

Whyte, William F., *Organizational Behavior: Theory and Applications.* Homewood, Ill.: Richard D. Irwin, Inc., 1969.

Winter, Gibson, *Religious Identity: The Organization of the Major Faiths.* Macmillan Inc., 1968.

Planning
(Chapters 2 and 3)

Allen, Roland, *The Spontaneous Expansion of the Church.* Grand Rapids: Wm. B. Eerdmans Publishing Company, 1962.

Barr, Browne, *Parish Back Talk.* Nashville: Abingdon Press, 1964.

Broholm, Richard R., *Strategic Planning for Church Organizations.* Valley Forge: Judson Press, 1969.

Brunner, Emil, *The Understanding of the Church.* London: Lutterworth Press, 1952.

Cavert, Samuel McCrea, *The American Churches in the Ecumenical Movement 1900-1968.* New York: Association Press, 1968.

Clark, M. Edward et al., eds., *The Church Creative.* Nashville: Abingdon Press, 1967.

Ewing, David W., *The Practice of Planning.* New York: Harper & Row, Publishers, Inc., 1968.

Fisher, Wallace, E., *From Tradition to Mission.* Nashville: Abingdon Press, 1965.

Gardner, E. Clinton, *The Church As a Prophetic Community.* Philadelphia: The Westminster Press, 1967.

Harrison, Paul M., *Authority and Power in the Free Church Tradition: A Social Case Study of the American Baptist Convention.* Carbondale, Ill.: Southern Illinois University Press, 1971.

Judy, Marvin, *The Cooperative Parish in Nonmetropolitan Areas.* Nashville: Abingdon Press, 1967.

Lee, Robert, *The Social Sources of Church Unity.* Nashville: Abingdon Press, 1960.

Leiffer, Murray H., *The Effective City Church,* 2d. rev. ed. Nashville: Abingdon Press, 1961.

Maring, Norman H., and Hudson, Winthrop S., *A Baptist Manual of Polity and Practice.* Valley Forge: Judson Press, 1963.

Marty, Martin E.; Rosenberg, Stuart E.; and Greely, Andrew M., *What Do We Believe? The Stance of Religion in America.* New York: Hawthorn Books, Inc., 1968.

Mead, Sidney E., *The Lively Experiment: The Shaping of Christianity in America.* New York: Harper & Row, Publishers, Inc., 1963.

Moberg, David O., *The Church As a Social Institution.* Englewood Cliffs, N. J.: Prentice-Hall, Inc., 1962.

Moore, Richard E., and Day, D. L., *Urban Church Breakthrough.* New York: Harper & Row, Publishers, Inc., 1966.

Niebuhr, H. Richard, *The Social Sources of Denominationalism.* New York: Holt, Rinehart & Winston, 1929.

Pfeffer, Leo, *Creeds in Competition.* New York: Harper & Row, Publishers, Inc., 1958.

Schaller, Lyle E., *Parish Planning.* Nashville: Abingdon Press, 1971.

Schaller, Lyle E., *Local Church Looks to the Future.* Nashville: Abingdon Press, 1968.

Financial Management
(Chapter 4)

Brigham, Eugene F., and Ricks, R. Bruce, *Readings in Essentials of Managerial Finance*. New York: Holt, Rinehart & Winston, Inc., 1968.

Davis, William, *The Language of Money: An Irreverent Dictionary of Business and Finance*. Boston: Houghton Mifflin Company, 1973.

Ellis, Loudell O., *Church Treasurer's Handbook*. Valley Forge: Judson Press, 1978.

Gross, Malvern J. Jr., *Financial and Accounting Guide for Nonprofit Organizations*. New York: Ronald Press Company, 1972.

McLeod, Thomas E., *The Work of the Church Treasurer*. Valley Forge: Judson Press, 1981.

Novick, David, *Current Practices in Program Budgeting*. New York: Crane, Russack & Co., Inc., 1973.

Church Marketing
(Chapter 5)

	Marketing Activity
Babbie, Earl R., *Survey Research Methods*. Belmont, Calif.: Wadsworth Publishing Company, Inc., 1973.	Information Acquisition
Churchill, Gilbert A., Jr., *Marketing Research: Methodological Foundations*. Hinsdale, Ill.: Dryden Press, 1976.	Information Acquisition
Cutlip, Scott M., and Center, Allen H., *Effective Public Relations*, 4th ed. Englewood Cliffs, N. J.: Prentice-Hall, Inc., 1971.	Information Supply
Engel, James F., and Norton, Wilbert H., *What's Gone Wrong with the Harvest?* Grand Rapids, Mich.: Zondervan Corporation, 1975.	Information Supply
Ferber, Robert A., *Handbook of Marketing Research*. New York: McGraw-Hill, Inc., 1974.	Information Acquisition
Gaedeke, R. M., *Marketing in Private and Public Nonprofit Organizations: Perspectives and Illustrations*. Santa Monica, Calif.: Goodyear Publishing Co., Inc., 1977	General

Goodman, Charles S., *Management of the Personal Selling Function.* New York: Holt, Rinehart & Winston, 1971.   Information Supply

Kotler, Philip, *Marketing for Nonprofit Organizations.* Englewood Cliffs, N. J.: Prentice-Hall, Inc., 1975.   General

————, "Strategies for Introducing Marketing into Nonprofit Organizations," *Journal of Marketing,* vol. 43, no. 1 (January, 1979), pp. 37-44.   Marketing Organization

————, and Levy, Sidney J., "Broadening the Concept of Marketing," *Journal of Marketing,* vol. 33, no. 1 (January, 1969), pp. 10-15.   General

Roman, Kenneth, and Maas, Jane, *How to Advertise.* New York: St. Martin's Press, Inc., 1977.   Information

Rothschild, Michael L., "Marketing Communications in Nonbusiness Situations or Why It's So Hard to Sell Brotherhood Like Soap," *Journal of Marketing,* vol. 43, no. 2 (Spring, 1979), pp. 11-20.   Information Supply

Sharpiro, Benson, "Marketing for Nonprofit Organizations," *Harvard Business Review,* vol. 51, no. 5 (September-October, 1973), pp. 123-132.   General

Implications of the Future
(Appendix)

Barbour, Ian G., *Myths, Models, and Paradigms: A Comparative Study in Science and Religion.* New York: Harper and Row, Publishers, Inc., 1974.

Bell, Daniel, ed., *Toward the Year 2000: Work in Progress.* Boston: Houghton Mifflin Company, 1968.

————, *The Coming of Post-Industrial Society: A Venture in Social Forecasting.* New York: Basic Books, Inc., Publishers, 1973.

Berry, Adrian, *The Next Ten Thousand Years: A Vision of Man's Future in the Universe.* New York: American Elsevier Publishers, Inc., 1974.

Bright, James, *Technological Forecasting for Industry and Government: Methods and Applications.* Englewood Cliffs, N. J.: Prentice-Hall, Inc., 1968.

Clarke, Arthur, *Profiles of the Future*. New York: Harper & Row, Publishers, Inc., 1963.

Cleveland, Harlan, *The Future Executive: A Guide for Tomorrow's Managers*. New York: Harper and Row, Publishers, Inc., 1972.

Cornish, E., *The Study of the Future*. Washington, D. C.: World Future Society, 1976.

Drucker, Peter, *The Age of Discontinuity: Guidelines to Our Changing Society*. New York: Harper & Row, Publishers, Inc., 1969.

Farmer, Richard N., *The Real World of 1984: A Look at the Foreseeable Future*. New York: David McKay Co., Inc., 1973.

Ferkiss, Victor, *The Future of Technological Civilization*. New York: George Braziller, Inc., 1974.

Gabor, Dennis, *Inventing the Future*. New York: Alfred A. Knopf, Inc., 1964.

Hesburgh, Theodore M., *The Humane Imperative: A Challenge for the Year 2000*. New Haven: Yale University Press, 1974.

Kahn, Herman, and Bruce-Briggs, Barry, *Things to Come: Thinking About the Seventies and Eighties*. New York: Macmillan, Inc., 1972.

Mead, Shepherd, *How to Get to the Future Before It Gets to You*. New York: Hawthorn Books, Inc., 1974.

Polak, Fred, *The Image of the Future*. San Francisco: Jossey-Bass, Inc., Publishers, 1972.

Index

A, B, C priority system, 165, 168
action plan, 25, 29, 34, 44, 58, 159,
    166-167, 168, 169
action steps, 39, 40, 45
activity, 37, 59, 62, 161, 165
annual plans, communications tool, 44
annual plans, cross analysis, 42
annual plans, development, 40
annual plans, evaluation process, 42,
    44, 48
annual plans, program targets, 40, 42
annual plans, purposes, 39, 47
annual plans vs. budget, 40, 44, 54-55
audit, administrative, 9, 147, 149-154
authority, 11, 12, 13, 14, 131, 135-138,
    140, 148

budget vs. financial pledging, 46-47

canvass director, 60-61, 67
canvass plan, 57, 67
cash flow, 70
church programs, 28, 29, 34, 39, 89,
    93, 95, 148, 155
church resource checklist, 27-28
communications, expectations and
    perceptions, 14, 17, 18
communications, with lay leaders, 14,
    18
congregational profile, 27, 83-84, 90-
    91
consistency, 54
cross-impact analysis, 179, 180, 182

daily scheduling, 168-169
differentiated marketing, 87, 94
discretionary expenditures, 59, 60, 62
discretionary time, 157
distribution strategy, 86
documentation, 79

employee compensation, 104
employee performance appraisal, 106,
    109
exception reporting, 73
exchange theory, 135, 140-141, 143-
    145
external environment analysis, 25-26,
    28-29, 45

financial control, 51
financial management, 51, 52
financial planning, 52, 80
functional expenses allocation, 56, 62
futures analysis, 179-182
futurism, 179-182

governing board, 13, 40, 44, 47, 55, 70,
    73, 100, 142, 149, 150, 176

image, 87-89, 94
information sources, 26-27
internal capability analysis, 25, 27-29,
    45
interruptions, 160-161
intersender conflict, 126
intrasender conflict, 125